# What's the Big Deal About JESUS?

## John Ankerberg & Dillon Burroughs

HARVEST HOUSE PUBLISHERS

EUGENE, OREGON

*Cover photo © Charles Taylor / iStockphoto*

*Cover by Dugan Design Group, Bloomington, Minnesota*

## WHAT'S THE BIG DEAL ABOUT JESUS?

Copyright © 2007 by John Ankerberg and Dillon Burroughs
Published by Harvest House Publishers
Eugene, Oregon 97402
www.harvesthousepublishers.com

Library of Congress Cataloging-in-Publication Data
    Ankerberg, John, 1945-
    What's the big deal about Jesus? / John Ankerberg and Dillon Burroughs.
        p. cm.
    Includes bibliographical references.
    ISBN-13: 978-0-7369-2120-6
    ISBN-10: 0-7369-2120-6
    1. Jesus Christ--Person and offices. 2. Apologetics. I. Burroughs, Dillon. II. Title.
    BT203.A55 2007
    232—dc22

                              2007006985

# Contents

## Part One: What Do We *Really* Know About Jesus?

## Part Two: Who Did Jesus Claim to Be?

## Part Three: Did Jesus Really Come Alive Again?

# How to
# Use This
# Book

**W**hat's the Big Deal About Jesus? is designed not only for *communication,* but also for building *community.* Developed around 13 of the core concepts utilized by experts to discuss the life of Jesus Christ, these chapters can stand as the basis of a small discussion group, classroom study, or retreat resource for those desiring to share their learning with others.

At the end of this book you'll find a discussion guide. Feel free to use these questions as starting points for even further discussion as you seek to find Jesus' relevance for today.

Throughout the pages of this resource, you'll also notice that many of the statistics and detailed quotes are placed in various sidebars. We've intentionally done this to help the text of the book feel more like a conversation. However, we still feel passionate about providing additional research for those desiring more information. We hope that these quotes, statistics, and insights will help supercharge your growth even further.

Third, you'll also find a wide variety of further materials in the "Additional Resources" section—materials that will enhance your understanding of these issues concerning Jesus. We've mentioned other books we've written regarding Jesus, several top Web sites that are good for personal study, and links to the best online articles from the Ankerberg Theological Research Institute. In addition, we've listed all the related video series and transcripts from past episodes of *The John Ankerberg Show* for those who prefer to use audio-visual resources.

Also, we are glad to personally be involved in the learning process with you. Feel free to contact us via e-mail (bigdealaboutjesus@ ankerberg.org) or regular mail with any comments or questions you may have.

Finally, know we are praying with you as you progress in your understanding of the "big deal" about Jesus today. We hope your desire to learn matches that of the Bereans in Paul's day. They searched the scriptures every day to discover whether what they were learning was true. God bless you as you discover (or rediscover) the big deal about Jesus!

# Why Should I Care About Jesus?

*"If he's a healer, why is there pain?*

*If he's really there, why do I feel so alone?*

*If he really cares, why doesn't he do something to show me?*

*If he really is all-powerful, why doesn't he do something to prove it?"*

*"Why should I care about Jesus?*

*Even if he did live, do miracles, heal the sick,*

*and even raise from the dead, why should it matter to me?"*

Talking about Jesus today can be hazardous to your health. In over 30 countries, a person can be arrested, tortured, or even killed for choosing to follow Jesus Christ. In contrast, Western culture enjoys religious freedom. We do not usually experience such treatment from the government when we speak out about our religious beliefs. Yet controversy still exists.

For instance, in March 2007, *Discovery* Channel aired a television special called "The Lost Tomb of Jesus," which claimed that Jesus, his mother Mary, and even his alleged spouse Mary Magdalene and son Jude were all buried in a tomb in the Talpiot section of Jerusalem. The show was watched by over four million viewers, and the corresponding book, *The Jesus Family Tomb Controversy*, rocketed onto the New York Times best-seller list.[1]

And in 2006, in Fredrickson, Virginia, a city council member came under legal pressure for offering a prayer "in Jesus name" during a meeting because it was against the council's policy for prayer to be offered in the name of "any particular deity." The Fredericksburg city council's policy prohibiting sectarian prayers was adopted after the American Civil Liberties Union of Virginia threatened them with a lawsuit if they did not take steps to pressure or force the council member to stop praying in Jesus Christ's name.[2]

Why such controversy? In a word—*Jesus.*

## Jesus' Story

Jesus of Nazareth transformed history as we know it. Our thinking, our beliefs, our education system, the fields of medicine, science, mathematics, law, and more—almost every area of our lives—have been touched by his hand in some way.

Did you know that followers of Jesus...

> ...founded Harvard, Princeton, Yale, and dozens of other prestigious American universities?
>
> ...helped author the U.S. Constitution?
>
> ...served as significant figures in the development of Western philosophy?
>
> ...provided assistance in abolishing slavery in England and America?
>
> ...pursued education and equal rights for women?
>
> ...have opened thousands of orphanages worldwide?

...continue to lead the world in private charitable giving to humanitarian needs?

While many reject the influence of Christianity in their lives today, they cannot reject that the Christian faith has influenced major segments of our culture. If for no other reason, they should care about Jesus simply because of his influence in the world around us.

However, a much more significant reason serves as the motivation for this book. We hope you would also consider investigating Jesus *personally*. We desire for you not just to ask, "What's the big deal about Jesus?" but to also consider, "What is the big deal about Jesus *in my life?*"

In the upcoming pages, you'll find stories and information that help provide answers to the key spiritual questions about Jesus. Please remember that the purpose of this book is not so much to *convince* as much as it is to *assist* you. Our goal is not to criticize you but to converse with you.

We encourage you to brew a mug of your favorite coffee, grab a fresh bagel, and join us for a look at who Jesus really was and is. And in the course of this journey, we hope you'll consider how the story of Jesus connects with your story. Perhaps both of your stories will converge as you take the steps of discovery essential to your own spiritual growth.

## Our Stories

Before we share together in this spiritual quest, we want to be up front and share our own stories and how they connect with Jesus. You may be surprised at how our spiritual progress was not as smooth or instantaneous as some might think.

### John's Story

From an early age, I can remember my father traveling around the world to speak with students about Jesus. One of my early memories is traveling to Sweden with him at the age of five as he spoke to audiences through an interpreter. He served in an organization called Youth for Christ, which at the time, included Billy Graham, Torrey Johnson, Merv Roselle, and Bob Pierce (the founder of World Vision). I literally grew up with these men spending time in my family's Chicago home.

During my adolescent years I took a class with a 16-year-old guy who told me what it meant to know God personally. But the idea both delighted and frightened me. Would God really accept me just as I was? After a week of struggling through my doubts, I prayed and invited Jesus into my life. I can vividly remember the joy and forgiveness I experienced that day.

Two years later I became extremely sick and was rushed to a hospital. I thought for certain I would die when I heard the doctor who was making the house call say, "We don't have time to call an ambulance. He needs to be operated on immediately. I'll take him in my car." I prayed to Jesus for help, and even today I can still recall the overwhelming peace that flooded my young body. In the worst of situations, Jesus provided hope. In the end, I survived, and I was determined to continue following the One who gave me strength.

When I entered high school, I decided to carry my Bible with me. It instantly became a magnet. Students had questions, and I shared how my life had been changed. Students asked *more* questions, and I would go home each night and look for the answers to what my friends asked about God. The next day I would return and share what I had discovered.

By the time I finished high school, the little Bible club I had helped to begin had grown to over 400 students each week. It was one of the largest Bible clubs in the nation at the time. The group included my high school buddies Jerry Jenkins, who would go on to coauthor the bestselling Left Behind series with Tim LaHaye, and Bruce Barnes (who later served as a missionary and was included as a character in the Left Behind books).

I attended college at the University of Illinois-Chicago Circle campus. Many well-meaning people told me I would lose my faith in a public university. Instead, I became the leader of the campus InterVarsity Christian Fellowship group and began once again to encourage students to look to Jesus and the Bible for answers to the issues in their lives, just as I had done in high school.

After I finished college I went on to graduate school. During that time, I traveled to college campuses around the nation as a speaker, seeking to provide answers to questions that students had about the Christian faith. I also married Darlene, and soon we had a beautiful daughter, Michelle. In time, I finished graduate school and received degrees in ministry, church history, and the philosophy of Christian thought.

Then God did something unexpected. A friend of mine had started a Christian television station in Kansas City and asked me to do a program. I agreed, and invited both Christian and non-Christian guests to respond to the question, "What do you believe, and why do you believe it?" This interview-style approach was completely new to Christian television at the time and opened a new way for me to share my faith with others. This first series soon led to the program being picked up nationwide as a weekly show, which is now in all 50 states and broadcast in dozens of countries around the world.

Over the past 27 years I've invited well-known non-Christian guests to discuss issues with Christian guests, including atheists such as Paul Kurtz (author of the *Humanist Manifesto II)* and Antony Flew (at the time considered the world's leading philosophical atheist). I've also interviewed leaders in other world religions and new religious movements, as well as key Christian individuals who are experts in fields such as science, theology, medicine, and history. Repeatedly, my experience has been that Christianity is true and can defend itself in the arena of the world's ideas.

Do I face challenges and problems? Yes, just like everyone else. This past year, for example, when I wasn't feeling well, I visited my doctor so he could run some tests. To my surprise, he reported that I had severely blocked arteries and had possibly experienced a minor heart attack. I would need surgery almost immediately.

While getting over my initial shock, I prayed as I had many years before as a young child facing physical tragedy. God reminded me of two key promises at that time: "I will never leave or forsake you," and "I can do all things through Christ who strengthens me." I sensed the same peace I did as a teen when I prepared to enter surgery—the kind of peace only God can provide.

Over five hours later, I was told the doctor had performed an astounding *ten bypasses* on my heart. I didn't even know that was possible! When the doctor drew a diagram of the work he had done, it looked as if he had completely rewired my heart. God had answered my prayers and given my heart new life.

In our television ministry today, the equipment we use is dramatically different from what we had in earlier years. We no longer need an enormous mound of electrical gear to produce a show. We can now edit everything on one computer, with top-quality results. And instead of typing up a book on a typewriter, I collaborate on books via laptops and digital voice recorders. Our ministry also offers digital downloads of programs that can be viewed instantly—a huge change from cassettes sent by mail.

Despite the technological changes, the message has stayed consistent. From my childhood to now, the life-altering reality that Jesus is a big deal, that he rose from the dead, and that he is God's son forms the foundation for my life and work.

### Dillon's Story

I'm 31 years old, married, have two kids, and am actively involved in my church. I like to play guitar, drink coffee with friends at Starbucks, and write. I grew up in a two-parent, two-income family. My dad worked in construction as a concrete finisher. My mom labored through a conglomeration of jobs over the years to help pay the bills. I attended public schools, rode the bus, played football and basketball, and played the saxophone in band.

Like many teenagers, I didn't care too much about Jesus until my life was a wreck. Even though my family attended a small church in the area, it wasn't until just before my senior year of high school that

I made a deliberate decision to follow Jesus Christ. I had repeated the prayers and raised my hand at the right times at church, but going through the *motions* was not changing my *emotions*. My way of life definitely wasn't working; I thought I might as well try his.

When I began my senior year of high school and told my principal I wanted to start a Bible study that would meet each morning before school, he nearly fell out of his chair! It was the first time I had ever been to his office without breaking some major rule. By the end of the year, however, several of my friends and I were meeting together every day at 7:30 a.m. In May of that year, my school principal even attended a prayer event we sponsored on the morning of the National Day of Prayer.

College was a challenge, to say the least. It seems as though I changed majors about as often as I did laundry for the first couple of years, finally choosing a "marketable" major called communications. I figured that because "excellent communication skills" was a requirement in virtually every job ad, majoring in the subject couldn't hurt.

But another big change happened before my senior year of college. Through a bizarre sequence of events, I ended up as an intern with Campus Crusade for Christ, a ministry committed to helping students live out their Christian faith on campus. We just called it "Cru"—nothing fancy, just some students trying to figure out life and God. The group quickly grew to well over 50 students during that year, making it one of the largest Christian groups on our campus at the time. My communication skills were now serving a higher purpose.

After much prayer and some advice from my friend Gabe, my wife, Deborah, and I finished our schooling and headed from small-town Indiana to downtown Dallas, Texas. We lived in an undersized apartment four blocks from Baylor Hospital. Though the location was great, it was dreadfully noisy when an ambulance sped by at 3:00 in the morning. Despite the broken sleep patterns, I became a "master of theology" in three quick years while working for various Christian organizations.

After receiving my degree, I headed north of downtown to serve at a medium-sized Bible church and lead teenagers and college students. Unlike any other time in my life, my beliefs were challenged as I dealt with everything from teen suicide to juvenile offenders to straight-A students who struggled with doubts about their faith. A teenager catching her dad viewing porn was never discussed in church history. A mom calling at 11:00 p.m. because she couldn't find her daughter had not been addressed in any of my textbooks. I learned how to serve the way Jesus did—by helping those in need. Through the ups and downs, those church friends became family, providing relationships I cherish to this day.

Fast-forward to today. My gorgeous wife, Deborah, and I have two awesome kids, Ben and Natalie. A major portion of each day is invested in writing or editing projects for various Christian authors. But by no means am I saying that I've arrived. My personal struggles still continue at times. Like every other breathing person, I question how God can be at work in the death of a family member. Doubts linger when my bank account runs low. Along the way, I've discovered that following Jesus is certainly not boring. It's an adventure for those who choose it.

My prayer is that as you continue through this book, you will do so with a mind that is curious rather than rejecting. I hope we can engage in conversation.

The other day, my favorite Starbucks barista, Rob, asked me how my writing was going. I told him I owed him a copy of this book because I had written every word of it while sitting in his café. Why? For one, it's the cheapest office space in town. But another reason is that, as I write, I've found it helpful to imagine I'm sitting across the coffee table from someone and talking about the important issues of life. "How's work? How's school? How's the family?"

I also hope to encourage you with questions of the heart, just as Jesus did—questions such as, "How is your spiritual life? How is your heart?" If you haven't stopped to think about these matters of the soul recently, I invite you to begin, sit back, and reflect as you read these words and consider what they mean to you.

Along the way, feel free to send us an e-mail with any comments or questions you have. We'll personally respond to you as soon as we are able. Just send your e-mail to staff@johnankerberg.org. That's all it takes.

## A Journey of a Thousand Miles

There's an oft-quoted Chinese proverb that says, "The journey of a thousand miles begins with one step." This statement is certainly true when it comes to learning about Jesus. More books have probably been written about him than any figure in history—too many for any one person to even begin to read or comprehend. As we begin our journey, we encourage you to take it one step at a time, seeking the truth about Jesus and how it impacts your life today.

**Part One:**

# What Do We *Really* Know About Jesus?

*"The alleged gospel writers—Matthew, Mark, Luke and John—describe a series of events that never happened a long time ago, in the life of a person that never lived a long time ago....The biblical Jesus is by and large a fabrication—one that is perfectly innocent and understandable but is still a fabrication."*

—MARCUS BORG, IN *MEETING JESUS AGAIN FOR THE FIRST TIME*[1]

*"When we are children and don't know what to do, what do we do? We turn to our parents. Everyone wants to believe they have the truth, and everyone can come to believe that what they believe is right, but that doesn't mean it is."*

—COMMENT FROM A MYSPACE.COM BLOG

**M**yspace.com offers anyone with an online connection the ability to voice his or her opinion on any issue. As part of the research for this book, we asked various myspace.com viewers to share their thoughts about Jesus. We did not limit the invitation to people of any particular age group or religious affiliation. Anyone who wanted to answer could do so. We asked them for questions they wanted to ask Jesus, and their replies spoke volumes. Some questions they wanted to ask included:

- How do you decide who is in and who is out?
- I believe in a higher being, but who is to say which god is right?
- Did you "hook up" with Mary Magdalene?
- How do you view the other religions out there?
- What are your views about the war in Iraq?
- Why are you still allowing so much suffering in the world?

One observation we made is that many of the questions don't doubt that Jesus existed. Rather, they doubt what we can actually *know* about Jesus. In other words, even if I believe Jesus did or does exist, how do I decide what is *true* about him? Is Jesus just "my homeboy," like the T-shirt portrays, only slightly more religious than us? Or is he something more? Is his life simply a fabrication, as scholars like Marcus Borg have suggested? Or is he really the Son of God?

The next four chapters answer these questions from four different angles. The first question we'll consider is, "What did his friends say about him?" In other words, we'll hear from the people who were closest to Jesus—those who would be the most likely to know the most about him and his life. What did people like Matthew, Mark, Luke, John, and Paul—all of whom walked with Jesus or were alive during his lifetime—say about him? The material we have from these friends includes the books traditionally labeled the four Gospels—Matthew, Mark, Luke, and John—and the letters of the apostle Paul. Their stories reveal a detailed picture of the one whom they believed was the Messiah.

After that, we'll take a look at what *other people* said about Jesus during his lifetime. In other words, if Jesus really healed people, raised the dead, and gathered huge crowds, certainly *others* would have left records of such activities. They did. We'll check out what their documents say about Jesus and his early followers. Many of these sources were written by non-Christians, too, making for an interesting look from early skeptics.

As we dialogue about the life of Jesus, we can't leave out his culture. Do the findings strengthen what others have said about Jesus, or do they contradict them? In chapter 3 we'll look at some of the archaeological finds from Jesus' time and discover what perspectives they offer to our understanding of him.

Then we'll address one of the most controversial issues regarding the early accounts of Jesus—the reliable transmission of the New Testament documents in the early church. In other words, even if Jesus' friends did record an accurate story, how do we know that *what we have is what they wrote?*

As you read along, you may want to have a pen handy so you can mark statements that stand out to you or write some of your own questions in the margins. Check out the endnotes that appear in the back of this book for Internet links and other books that relate to the discussion at hand. You can also e-mail any questions or thoughts you have—just send them to bigdealaboutjesus@johnankerberg.org. We look forward to hearing about how this information encourages you and helps answer the questions you have about Jesus.

The Biographies of Jesus:

# What Did His
**1** | **Friends Say?**

I magine having a close friend from your high school years killed in a tragic automobile accident. Many who also attended the same school turn out for the funeral, and some of them share why he was such a wonderful person. They recall some of the sports teams he was involved with, and recount many of his acts of kindness. For days afterward, you talk with many others about his life.

A few years later, as you're sitting down one night looking at old pictures, you decide to write a book about your friend. After your book is published, to your astonishment, some people say it's inaccurate and that you *forgot* key details about your friend's life. They say he *wasn't* on any sports teams, *wasn't* involved in the acts of kindness you mentioned, and *didn't* die in a car accident. How would you respond?

You could gather other voices of support. There would be other athletes from the school teams who could testify he did play on those teams. Those whom your friend visited in hospitals could recall how his visits cheered them up. Medical records could testify that he really was killed in a car accident. Your friend left behind a trail of information that confirms the details in your book.

Jesus' friends encountered a similar problem.

After Jesus was murdered, his friends gathered behind locked doors, fearing persecution from those who had helped put Jesus to death. But that changed when Jesus came back from the dead and showed his followers that he had conquered death. He commanded them to communicate this good news they had seen to others. They did.

A few years later, some of these followers sat down and wrote four books about him, sharing the stories of Jesus' life. But after those books (called the Gospels) were written, some people began to doubt them. And that problem has persisted through today.

## Christianity Before the New Testament

People commonly ask today:

- Isn't it likely that the Gospel writers simply forgot many details about what Jesus said and did by the time they wrote their books?

- Since the Gospels were written by people who followed Jesus, how can we be sure their faith didn't get in the way of what they wrote?

- How do we know the Gospel writers didn't invent a new Jesus who would be "more appealing" to people?

- Why did they wait so long before they wrote about Jesus' life?

These are all good questions and can be answered by looking at the historical record of what happened.

We must remember that what was important to the apostles and the early Christians was communicating the good news about Jesus. The apostles had spent three years living with him, and when he came back to life, he told them how to talk about him to other people. Jesus commanded them to "go into all the world and preach the gospel."[2]

*The First 50 Days*

Luke records the official start of the church in the book of Acts, which was written by about A.D. 63. Fifty days after Jesus rose from the dead in approximately A.D. 30, Luke records that the apostles preached to devout Jews from different parts of the world who had made the pilgrimage to Jerusalem to celebrate Pentecost.[3] The apostle Peter addressed these people and proclaimed the facts about Jesus' life, death, and resurrection. As a result, 3,000 Jews believed the message and joined the Christian movement. These people stayed in Jerusalem for a brief period, where they "devoted themselves to the apostles' teaching and to the fellowship, to the breaking of bread and to prayer."[4] Many then returned to their own nations. It is important to realize that the message the apostles preached 50 days after the resurrection was the same message these people preached across the Roman Empire. This A.D. 30 message that was shared over the next 40 years was not forgotten, didn't change, and went back to Jesus himself.

So here we find that within two months of Jesus' death and resurrection, a large number of believers have emerged. Many of them went on to travel throughout the Roman Empire to spread the message of Jesus. Luke lists the nations as including "Parthians, Medes and Elamites; residents of Mesopotamia, Judea and Cappadocia, Pontus and Asia, Phrygia and Pamphylia, Egypt and the parts of Libya near Cyrene; visitors from Rome (both Jews and converts to Judaism); Cretans and Arabs."[5] At least 15 different people groups outside of Jerusalem spread the foundational truths of Christianity almost immediately after the events in Acts 2 occurred.

### The First Few Years

Shortly after this amazing gathering in Jerusalem, Luke records that "more and more men and women believed in the Lord and were added to their number."[6] The result was that "the word of God spread [throughout Jerusalem and into the regions beyond]. The number of disciples in Jerusalem increased rapidly, and a large number of priests became obedient to the faith."[7] This growth included Jewish priests in Jerusalem who accepted the preaching of the apostles and began to follow the teachings of Jesus.

The early church leaders made it a priority to communicate about Jesus by word of mouth. The rapid gain of many new converts and the starting of new church congregations and other events were happening so quickly that the earliest Christian leaders didn't initially pause to write down an authoritative compilation of Christ's life. Luke recorded that at the time of his writing, there were many eyewitness reports circulating.[8] Some believe Luke's gospel even included interviews with Mary, the mother of Jesus and other family members and close friends. Even written records would not have been uncommon, since many Jews in that time took down notes from the messages of popular rabbis and teachers.

Any question that needed an answer could often be directed to one of the apostles or numerous eyewitnesses to the resurrected Jesus. The remarkable speed with which Christianity spread throughout the Roman Empire within the lifetimes of the apostles is evidence of the early success in conveying the message by word of mouth.

Dr. N.T. Wright, Bishop of Durham and former professor of New Testament at Oxford, explained in an interview on *The John Ankerberg Show* that

> in A.D. 20 there's no such a thing as a Christian church. By A.D. 120, the emperor in Rome is getting worried letters from one of his proconsuls in northern Turkey about what to do about these Christians. So in that one century, you have this extraordinary thing suddenly appearing out of nowhere. All the early Christians for whom we have actual evidence would say, "I'll tell you why it's happened. It's because of Jesus of Nazareth and the fact that he was raised from the dead."[9]

Additional evidence that the message of Christ spread quickly across the Roman Empire after Jesus was crucified and rose again can be read in some of the apostles' letters. In some cases, they wrote to churches that had been established in far distant areas. For example:

- Before the apostle Paul visited the Christians in the church in Rome, he wrote (in about A.D. 57) and told them that "your faith is being reported all over the world."[10] Remember that according to Acts 2:10, there were some people from Rome at Pentecost. They would have returned to Rome to share their newfound truth with others.

- James, the brother of Jesus, wrote the book of James by the early 50s to early Jewish-Christian churches "scattered among the nations."[11]

- Peter wrote in the early 60s to Christians who were in churches "scattered throughout Pontus, Galatia, Cappadocia, Asia, and Bithynia."[12]

Long before the New Testament books were written, Christians across the Roman Empire already knew the facts about Jesus' life, death, and resurrection. Many became martyrs because they believed these facts and became his followers. It seems completely unreasonable to think that when the four Gospels were written only 30 to 50 years after Jesus' death and resurrection that they presented an entirely new Jesus—someone significantly different than the one the early Christians themselves had personally seen and heard.

### The Founding Sacraments

In addition, the Lord's Supper (also known as Eucharist or communion), which Jesus himself had instituted, would have been taught, passed on, and celebrated many times from the very first time Christians met together for worship. In that very ceremony Christians were commanded to remember Jesus' death and resurrection, as well as the meaning of these events—the gospel. The same can be said concerning baptism. If someone were to try to change the earliest proclamation about Jesus in later years, first-generation Christians would have known and rejected such changes. Once the story of Jesus had spread beyond Jerusalem, neither the apostles nor anyone else would have been in a position to alter it.

Those who argue that the Jesus portrayed in the Gospels is somehow different from the Jesus of history must assume that the apostles forgot about the details regarding the real Jesus within 50 days after his crucifixion and after having lived alongside him for a three-year period. Even then, the apostles were not the only eyewitnesses to Jesus' life. The well-researched book *Reinventing Jesus* states, "Hundreds of other followers of Jesus knew him well, had seen his miracles, and had heard his messages. What Jesus taught and what Jesus did were not things done in secret. This hypothesis is so full of holes that no scholar holds to it."[13]

## The Writings of Jesus' Friends

The writings of Jesus' friends traditionally include the four Gospels and, indirectly, the letters circulated by the apostle Paul. Combined, these writers authored nearly the entire contents of the New Testament, and these writings were in circulation during the time both Jesus' friends and enemies were still alive. This means any errors that appeared in these texts would have been quickly exposed and corrected.

### The Four Gospel Writers

What kind of books are the four Gospels? I (John) discussed this question in an interview with some of the top Jesus scholars of our time, who shared their perspectives on the four gospels regarding sources, bias, authorship, and the time of their writing.

*Sources:* In response to the question of whether we can trust the Gospel accounts of Jesus, Dr. Craig Evans, Payzant Distinguished Professor of New Testament at Acadia Divinity College in Wolfville, Nova Scotia, Canada, answered, "You begin with your oldest and most reliable sources. We have them. We have four Gospels in the New Testament...just because the New Testament Gospel writers have a theological interest and that's what drives them to tell the story of Jesus in the first place, that doesn't disqualify their writing. It doesn't make it suddenly unhistorical or of no value." For a scholar who belonged to the *National Geographic* "Dream Team" that researched the *Gospel of Judas,* has authored over 50 books on New Testament topics, and has lectured at universities such as Cambridge, Durham, Oxford, and Yale, this is a profound statement.

Dr. Claire Pfann, professor at the University of the Holy Land in Jerusalem, shared in the same interview that "if we want to deal with the historicity of Jesus, then we have to immerse ourselves into the tools for examining that. That includes the Gospels, the literary texts, extrabiblical writings of other Jewish authors like Josephus, archaeology, and a study of biblical languages."

## When and Where Were the Gospels Written?

**Matthew:** Written by the apostle Matthew, probably from Antioch, Syria, in A.D. 50 or 60.

**Mark:** Written by John Mark, a companion of the apostle Peter, likely between A.D. 65–70. Papias, an early church leader who personally knew some of the apostles, wrote around 125–140 that "Mark, having become the interpreter of Peter, wrote down accurately, though not in deed or order, whatsoever he [Peter] remembered of the things said or done by Christ."

**Luke:** Written by Luke, a doctor and missionary friend of the apostle Paul, between A.D. 59–63, likely while in Rome, before the book of Acts and Paul's second imprisonment in A.D. 64.

**John:** John, like Matthew, was an eyewitness and a personal friend of Jesus. This Gospel was written between A.D. 70–98, most likely while John was leading the church in Ephesus.

*Bias:* Dr. Craig Blomberg, New Testament professor at Denver Seminary, noted that "in the ancient world nobody had yet invented the notion of objective, dispassionate chronicling of history simply for history's sake. They wouldn't bother to retell the story to somebody if they didn't feel there was something that could be learned from it."

Dr. Darrell Bock, a New Testament professor at Dallas Theological Seminary, agreed. "You can have history and theology together. Just think of the word *perspective* instead of *theology.* What the Gospels give us is the perspective of the disciples and those who believed Jesus in terms of what he did and said."

*Authorship:* Dr. Blomberg observed, "The sum total of the evidence that we have from the early church fathers is that the four men, Matthew, Mark, Luke, and John, to whom the New Testament is typically ascribed to...are in fact the people who wrote the stories about Jesus."

*Time of Writing:* Dr. Evans stated, "I would put the gospel writings around 35 to 50 years after Jesus' death....The books were written within the lifetimes of eyewitnesses."

According to Dr. Blomberg, "It wasn't just Christians who checked up on what was being said. There were plenty of hostile eyewitnesses to the life of Jesus, particularly in Israel, who if the first apostles had gone around saying anything substantially different from what others knew Jesus did and taught, would have been very happy to intervene."

These statements agree with even some liberal scholars, who, in recent years, have changed their opinions regarding the dates of New Testament books. For instance, William F. Albright wrote,

> We can already say emphatically that there is no longer any basis for dating any book of the New Testament after about A.D. 80, two full generations before the date between 130 and 150 given by the more radical New Testament critics of today....In my opinion, every book of the New Testament was written by a baptised Jew between the forties and eighties of the first century (very probably sometime between about A.D. 50 and 75).[14]

*What About Paul?*

There are some today who attempt to create a major distinction between the Jesus written about in the four Gospels and the Jesus written about by the apostle Paul. They claim that Paul taught a different message than the other apostles, even though they were all carrying on their ministries during the same time span and in the same geographic region. Yet the evidence shows this cannot be the case.

Historians generally agree that Paul wrote many of his letters before the four Gospels were produced. For example, Paul wrote a letter to the church at Corinth in about A.D. 55, within 25 years of the crucifixion of Jesus. In an interview I (John) conducted with New Testament historian Dr. Gary Habermas, Gary explained the importance of this letter.

> "The Gospels have all been called passion narratives with a long introduction. Almost half of the Gospels are spent on that last crucial, critical week of Jesus' life. Why is that? This is *prime time*. This is where the salvation of God, according to these witnesses, is actually being wrought. Could the world have been saved if Jesus never told the parable of the Good Samaritan? Of course. Could the world have been saved if blind Bartemaus had never received his sight? Of course. But what the early Christians did believe was that the world could not have been saved if Jesus had not come, if he had not died, and if he had not risen again."
>
> —DR. BEN WITHERINGTON ON
> *THE JOHN ANKERBERG SHOW*[15]

In his words, "In A.D. 30, Jesus died. Shortly thereafter, Peter, James, and the other apostles preached about Jesus' resurrection and deity. In A.D. 32 Paul meets the risen Christ on the road to Damascus. In A.D. 35 Paul goes to Jerusalem to meet the apostles Peter and James to see if his message contained the same truths about Christ that the other eyewitnesses of Jesus' life, death, and resurrection also preached. They tell him yes.

"Then in A.D. 51 Paul preaches to people in Corinth and many become Christians. In A.D. 55 Paul writes the book of 1 Corinthians and records the facts that he received from the other apostles about Jesus and knew to be true. This information [which must be dated within two years of Jesus' death and resurrection] shows Paul didn't invent Christ's deity, but that he was in agreement with the very same message that Peter and James preached. It is obvious that Peter and James were preaching their message way before Paul arrived on the scene."

What are the truths about Jesus that Peter, James, and the other apostles communicated before Paul became a Christian in about A.D. 32? Paul shared these truths in the following words. Note how he begins and ends:

> *For what I received I passed on to you* as of first importance: that Christ died for our sins according to the Scriptures, that he was buried, that he was raised on the third day according to the Scriptures, and that he appeared to Peter, and then to the Twelve. After that, he appeared to more than five hundred of the brothers at the same time, most of whom are still living, though some have fallen asleep. Then he appeared to James, then to all the apostles, and last of all he appeared to me also, as to one abnormally born....*Whether, then, it was I or they, this is what we preach,* and this is what you believed.[16]

According to what Paul wrote in Galatians,[17] Peter, James, and John confirmed Paul's teaching within *five years* of the occurrence of the events he wrote about. They were eyewitnesses of the risen Jesus, and they had taught these things from the time of the resurrection itself.

In such a short period of time, there is no way that legend or myth could develop and skew these facts. As Oxford historian A.N. Sherwin-White has written, "Legend takes at least two full generations [to develop], therefore no first-century data allows time for myths or legends to creep into the stories about Jesus."[18]

## What Did Jesus' Friends Say?

There are two general approaches to understanding what Jesus' friends said about him in the first four New Testament books. First, we can look for the similarities. Second, we can look for the differences. We're going to look at both, and begin with the common elements these four writers share.

### Consistent Historical Details

First, all four writers were consistent regarding the time period and locations in which Jesus lived. In other words, there was little controversy during their lifetimes that Jesus had actually been born in Bethlehem, moved to Egypt for a while, and then settled for most of his life in a small hill town called Nazareth. His traditional birth date of approximately 6–5 B.C. and death on Passover Day in the early A.D. 30s were not issues people of their time debated.

## The "Other" Friends of Jesus:

"The remarkable thing about Jesus is that he associated himself with the downtrodden, the unclean, the diseased, the outcasts of Jewish society—people who were regarded as morally and ritually unclean by the religious people of that time. This is highly significant in more than one way. Jesus' table fellowship with prostitutes and tax collectors and sinners was a way of saying the kingdom of God is open to you and you are welcome to come into it—to sit at a table with me and fellowship in the kingdom of God. But it was also an even deeper and more radical claim than that because by associating with such people, normally religious folk would have thought that Jesus made himself unclean. But in Jesus' eyes, it was just the opposite. Through contact with him, *they were made clean* so that it was his cleansing and forgiveness that was imparted to them rather than their contamination to him."

—DR. WILLIAM LANE CRAIG,
IN AN INTERVIEW ON *THE JOHN ANKERBERG SHOW*[19]

### The Phenomenon of Miracles

Second, each writer noted several miracles performed by Jesus. Luke, a medical doctor, shares several, while John describes only seven. Mark connects several short miracles in a row, apparently without much concern for chronological order, while Matthew prefers a more sequential treatment. According to their stories, even the Jews who doubted Jesus' claims that he was the Messiah agreed that great miracles were taking place. We'll talk more about this issue of miracles in chapter 5.

### The Death and Resurrection of Jesus

Third, all four Gospel writers agreed that Jesus died and came to life again. All four accounts describe a brutal death and multiple physical appearances of Jesus after his death. We'll talk more about these details later, but the point here is that we have four testimonies about a guy who comes back to life on his own.

We can talk about whether the writers were 100 percent accurate,[20] but it's hard to argue that there were any inconsistencies in these major areas. All four writers either lived as close friends with Jesus for over three years or wrote their accounts based on the reports of people who had been with Jesus. All four claimed the same facts about his life, his performance of supernatural acts, his violent death, and his coming back to life before returning to heaven.

## What Do These Writings Mean for Us Today?

You might be thinking, *Why does this even matter?* Look at it another way. If we, you, and two of your friends were to witness a car wreck, all five of us would likely be able to describe the accident accurately to a police officer a few minutes later. Each of us might forget some specific details next week or next year, but we would remember them right after the accident. If the person in the car were someone we knew from work or school, we would likely remember the event better even with the passage of time because we'll probably discuss the details again and again, perhaps even years later. But if the people in the car included *all five of us,* we would definitely remember the details of the incident for years to come. Why? Because it was *personal.* We were there!

Why do the writings of four men from the first century mean anything to us today? Because if Jesus *did* come back to life, then we should pay attention to what he had said. Maybe his teachings in the Jewish synagogues, his conversations with people on the street, and his preaching from a boat along the shore of the Sea of Galilee point not only to a good guy or even a prophet, but someone even more important.

That Jesus was a popular, controversial, and significant individual during his lifetime is indisputable. And we've seen what his friends had to say about him. But what about those *outside* of his circle of friends? How did *they* respond to his claims that he, a carpenter from a small town, was God's son? Hang on as we dig up the ancient thoughts of Jesus' cultural writers, media, and critics during the earliest years of the Christian movement.

The Media of Jesus:

# What Did Others
2 | # Say About Him?

**W**e live in a world of breaking news. As soon as a plane crashes, there is video of it on television. As soon as a key play ends a football game, it is instantly replayed everywhere. With the right tools we can even watch two or more channels at the same time and catch up on the latest stock prices from our mobile phones.

News didn't travel quite as quickly in the time of Jesus. Without television, Internet, radio, or overnight delivery, news traveled much slower—either by word of mouth or through the written word. The problem with word of mouth was that the facts could easily be altered. And the problem with the written word was that for centuries, all copying had to be completed by hand. This meant distribution was often slow and difficult.

Despite these primitive media tools, many newsworthy events that took place in the ancient world were preserved and have made their way down to us. Scribes and others regularly recorded daily affairs, current events, and legal activities. Ancient archives have been and continue to be discovered throughout the world in which Jesus lived, and these archives contain quotes from sources that accent and complement the claims of Jesus' friends.

In this chapter, we will walk through the known materials from the time of Jesus. Because there are several citations worth sharing, we've broken these up into three categories: secular Greco-Roman sources, non-Christian Jewish sources, and Christian sources.

---

### Ancient Evidence for the Life of Christ

According to Dr. Gary Habermas, there are 45 ancient sources about the life of Christ outside of the New Testament, including...

- 19 creedal statements

- 4 archaeological sources (such as stones, graves, tablets)

- 17 secular writings

- 5 extrabiblical Christian sources (early church fathers)

"Through this evidence we can substantiate 129 facts concerning the life, person, teachings, death, and resurrection of Jesus, plus the disciples' early message."[1]

---

## Secular Sources

While Christians left the 27 books of the New Testament and eight additional sources within the next generation, Roman sources left fewer works from this time period. However, many secular sources mentioned Jesus or Christianity within the first two centuries A.D. These include:

*Thallus (c. 50–75)*

Around 52, Thallus wrote a history of the Eastern Mediterranean world from the Trojan War to his time. Julius Africanus, writing in 221, quoted from this work by Thallus regarding the darkness that occurred at the time of Jesus' death. He wrote:

> On the whole world there pressed a most fearful darkness; and the rocks were rent by an earthquake, and many places in Judea and other districts were thrown down. This darkness Thallus, in the third book of his *History,* calls, as appears to me without reason, an eclipse of the sun.[2]

In this brief statement, we find talk of the crucifixion, the spread of the gospel in the Mediterranean region in the middle of the first century, and a record that skeptics offered rationalistic explanations for certain Christian teachings and supernatural claims.

### Pliny the Younger (c. 110)

Pliny was a Roman writer and administrator who served as the governor of Bithynia in Asia Minor (Turkey). In dealing with the persecution of Christians, he wrote:

> They—the Christians—were in the habit of meeting on a certain fixed day before it was light, when they sang in alternate verses a hymn to Christ, as to a God, and bound themselves by a solemn oath, not to any wicked deeds, but never to commit any fraud, theft or adultery, never to falsify their word, nor deny a trust when they should be called upon to deliver it up; after which it was their custom to separate, and then reassemble to partake of food—but food of an ordinary and innocent kind.[3]

Pliny confirms these facts found in the New Testament books:

- Christ was worshiped as deity by the first generation of Christians.
- Jesus' ethical teachings were reflected in the oath taken by Christians never to be guilty of a number of sins mentioned in the letter.
- We find a probable reference to communion in Pliny's remark about Christians gathering to partake of ordinary food.

### Tacitus (c. 115–120)

Cornelius Tacitus has been called the greatest historian of ancient Rome.[4] He was generally acknowledged among scholars for his moral integrity. In his *Annals* we find this entry:

Consequently, to get rid of the report, Nero fastened the guilt and inflicted the most exquisite tortures on a class hated for their abominations, called Christians by the populace. *Christus* [Christ], from whom the name had its origin, suffered the extreme penalty during the reign of Tiberius at the hands of one of our procurators, Pontius Pilate, and a most mischievous superstition [Christ's resurrection] thus checked for the moment, again broke out not only in Judea, the first source of the evil, but even in Rome, where all things hideous and shameful from every part of the world find their center and become popular.[5]

In this report we unearth six specific historical facts that agree with the New Testament:

1. Christians were named for their founder, *Christus* (Christ).

2. Christ was put to death by the Roman procurator Pontius Pilate.

3. This happened during the reign of Emperor Tiberius (between A.D. 14–37).

4. Christ's death ended the "superstition" [the resurrection] for a short time.

5. Christianity spread from Judea, from where it originated.

6. His followers carried this message to Rome.

### Why Aren't There *Earlier* Sources?

Yes, some of the writings shared here extend up to over a century after Jesus' death. We have to keep in mind that there are very few writings of any kind that still exist from the first century A.D. Wars, looting, fires, wear and tear, persecution, and even worms have destroyed many ancient scrolls and pages throughout the generations. It is interesting to note that according to more recent research, it has been observed that many Jewish and non-Jewish documents discovered up to A.D. 200 from the area where Jesus lived mention Jesus or Christianity. This is exactly the *opposite* of what many have traditionally questioned—"If Jesus was so important, why didn't more ancient writers mention him?" The answer is, *they did.*

### Suetonius (c. 117–138)

Suetonius was chief secretary to Emperor Hadrian of Rome and had access to Imperial records. Writing about 115, he noted, "Because the Jews at Rome caused continuous disturbances *at the instigation of Chrestus* [Christ], he expelled them from the city."[6] In another place, he spoke regarding Christians and stated, "After the great fire at Rome....Punishments were also inflicted on *the Christians, a sect professing a new and mischievous religious belief.*"[7]

His account includes three specific references to Christianity:

1. It was Jesus who caused the Jews to make an uproar in Rome.

2. Suetonius described Christianity's beliefs as mischievous—similar to how Tacitus refers to the concept of the resurrection.

3. Suetonius specifically used the term *Christians,* referring to them as those who followed the teachings of Christ.

### Lucian (c. 120–180)

Lucian, a second-century Greek satirist, spoke with disdain toward early Christians. Yet even in doing so he confirmed facts from the New Testament:

> The Christians, you know, worship a man to this day— the distinguished personage who introduced their novel rites, and was crucified on that account...and then it was impressed on them by their original law giver that they are all brothers, from the moment that they are converted, and deny the gods of Greece, and worshiped the crucified sage, and live after his laws.[8]

So in this mid-second century report, which was negative, we read that Christians worshiped a man named Jesus, a man who had been crucified. Upon conversion, these believers denied their former gods and followed Christ's teachings.

## Galen (c. 150)

Galen was a famous physician who lived in the second century. While his writings focus on medicine and the sciences, he includes four specific references to Christianity from Rome around 150, with the assumption that Christianity was already well known in the area by this time.[9]

## Celsus (c. 170)[10]

In *Against Celsus,* the early church father Origen quotes Celsus, a second-century skeptic, on Jesus. Apparently the teachings of Celsus had become quite problematic, as Origen argues against 17 specific arguments Celsus taught.[11]

Thus, every local and nearly all nonlocal sources from the time period comment on Jesus' existence or activities, indicating that Jesus at least lived as his friends claimed and operated in ways consistent with the secular sources.

## Jewish Sources

Jewish sources written during the first two centuries of Christianity include the works of a famous Jewish historian named Josephus and a collection of rabbinical writings known as the Talmud.

## Josephus (c. 37–97)

Josephus was born around the time Jesus died (A.D. 37) and wrote five major works, including a volume on the history of the Jews called *The Antiquities.* The English translation of his Greek masterpiece shares two significant sections on Jesus and Christianity. The shorter portion records:

[The high priest] convened the judges of the Sanhedrin, and brought before them the brother of Jesus, the one called Christ, whose name was James, and certain others, and accusing them of having transgressed the law delivered them up to be stoned.[12]

The reference here is clearly to James, brother of Jesus, who was put to death along with other Christians for their belief that Jesus was the Messiah.

When Peter escaped from jail, he shared with a group of believers, "Report these things to James and the brethren" (Acts 12:17 NASB).

Known as the leader of the first church in Jerusalem, James's death was a significant historical point for early Christianity—and apparently significant enough in secular culture to find a place in Josephus's account of Jewish history.

Josephus also mentions Jesus directly in one other place in *The Antiquities.* In an extended paragraph we find this:

Now there was about this time Jesus, a wise man, if it be lawful to call him a man; for he was a doer of wonderful works, a teacher of such men as receive the truth with pleasure. He drew over to him both many of the Jews and many of the Gentiles. He was [the] Christ. And when Pilate, at the suggestion of the principal men amongst us, had condemned him to the cross, those that loved him at the first did not forsake him; for he appeared to them alive again the third day; as the divine prophets had foretold these and ten thousand other wonderful things concerning him. And the tribe of Christians, so named from him, are not extinct to this day.

Some consider that the Christian references in this quote are later additions and should not be accepted as authentic. While there is question regarding the exact original Greek wording of this passage,

Shlomo Pines published a translation of a different version quoted in an Arabic manuscript of the tenth century. Its translation reads:

> At this time there was a wise man who was called Jesus, and his conduct was good, and he was known to be virtuous. And many people from among the Jews and the other nations became his disciples. Pilate condemned him to be crucified and to die. And those who had become his disciples did not abandon their loyalty to him. They reported that he had appeared to them three days after his crucifixion, and that he was alive. Accordingly they believed that he was the Messiah, concerning whom the Prophets have recounted wonders.

Pines suggests that this may be a more accurate record of what Josephus wrote, lacking the parts which have often been considered as later additions by Christian copyists. This would add weight to the argument that Josephus did write *something* about Jesus.

If this version is accurate, then the top Jewish historian of the first century made reference to Jesus and revealed that Jesus was part of the cultural history of Palestine. He details (regardless of which of the above versions is accepted) that:

- Jesus was known as a wise man.
- He had many followers among Jews and Gentiles.
- Pilate condemned him to death by crucifixion.
- Jesus' followers reported that he was alive again.
- Christians claimed that Jesus had appeared on the third day after his crucifixion.
- Christians believed that Jesus was the Messiah mentioned by the Old Testament prophets.

### The Talmud (compiled 70–200)

The Talmud was a collection of Jewish writings based on oral tradition extending back to the lifetime of Jesus. If you've read what the Jewish leaders claimed about Jesus in the Gospels, you already have a good idea of what the Talmud says about him. The Jewish leaders were not flattering and even accused Jesus of sorcery:

> ...on the eve of the Passover Yeshu [Jesus] was hanged [from the cross]. For forty days before the execution took place, a herald...cried, "He is going forth to be stoned because he has practiced sorcery and enticed Israel to apostasy."

This *Yeshu* was the Jewish name for Jesus. The word "hanged" is a symbolic reference to his execution, which the Gospel writers say came in the form of crucifixion. And the Jews *had* wanted to kill Jesus by stoning according to John 8:59, although they were not successful in this effort.

That Jewish writers of this time period—who were opposed to Jesus—would mention Jesus in these ways only helps confirm that what Jesus' friends said about him was true.

"The extrabiblical evidence [for Jesus] may not seem like much until we realize that ancient historians, for the most part, centered only on the lives and exploits of kings, of generals, of religious leaders in institutional positions of power, and that Jesus held none of these kinds of roles. In fact, it is only to the extent that he comes in contact with Herod or Pilate or the various ruling families that mention is made of him [in secular non-Christian sources]. From that point of view it is remarkable that we have any references to him at all in a period of time when people did not know the movement that would grow to universal proportions. But we certainly have enough information to know that he lived and to confirm the basic outline of the life of Christ from the Gospels."[13]

—DR. CRAIG BLOMBERG, PROFESSOR OF NEW TESTAMENT, DENVER THEOLOGICAL SEMINARY

## Christian Sources

Outside of the New Testament documents, of which several thousand early manuscript copies exist, a number of additional early Christian writings share information about Jesus and the early activities of his followers. The second generation of Christianity includes five specific sources supporting the original accounts written by Jesus' friends.[14]

### Clement (writing c. 95)

The earliest of these Christian writers was Clement, a leader in the church at Rome. In his letter to the Corinthian church around A.D. 95, he cites portions of Matthew, Mark, and Luke, where he introduces them as the actual words of Jesus.

---

#### Did You Know...

...both Clement and Papias are featured characters in the 2006 bestselling novel *John's Story* by Tim LaHaye and Jerry Jenkins? In this novel, Clement and Papias are found in Rome when John the apostle dictated his gospel and defended early Christianity against the early Gnostic teachings of Celsus.[15]

---

In other words, Clement lived in Rome in the years immediately following the deaths of the apostles Peter and Paul. He led a Christian church there and continued to communicate that the same Jesus they had been killed for had lived, died, and risen from the dead. Clement then declared that the accounts handed down in the Gospels by Jesus' friends were true.

### The Didache (c. 50–160)

Perhaps the second earliest Christian writing available outside of the New Testament authors is a document called the Didache ("the Teachings"). This document served as an ancient manual of Christianity that dates between the end of the first century to the beginning of the second century. It cites portions of the first three Gospels, referring to them as the words of Jesus with extensive quotes from Matthew.

---

#### "Why Are the Church Fathers Important?"

The church fathers were second- and third-generation believers of Christ's original followers. In addition to spreading the teachings as taught directly from the apostles, the church fathers helped affirm the acceptance and accuracy of the New Testament texts by referring to them frequently in their writings. For instance, Irenaeus (c. 170) quoted 23 of the 27 New Testament books less than 100 years after their writing, meaning he had access to these books *together* within a generation of the apostles. This would have been a tremendous accomplishment for a culture whose writings could be spread only through handwritten copies!

## Papias (writing c. 125–140)

Among other early Christian sources are the works of an early church leader named Papias. He served as a pastor at the church in Hierapolis, a town six miles north of Laodicea (on the Lycus River in modern-day western Turkey). It was a church founded as a result of Paul's missionary work,[16] and the church was traditionally believed to be led by the same Philip mentioned in Acts 6. This congregation continued to grow despite persecution through the early second century.

"Epaphras, who is one of you and a servant of Christ Jesus, sends greetings. He is always wrestling in prayer for you, that you may stand firm in all the will of God, mature and fully assured. I vouch for him that he is working hard for you and for those at Laodicea and Hierapolis."

—COLOSSIANS 4:12-13

Epaphras, a co-worker with the apostle Paul, assisted the church at Hierapolis in the A.D. 60s—the same church that Papias later served.

Papias circulated a collection of his sermons, titled the *Exposition of Oracles of the Lord,* around A.D. 130, in which he mentioned Matthew, Mark, Luke, and John as accepted and authentic works. He specifically referred to John's Gospel as containing the words of Jesus. For those seeking to discredit early Christianity, it is difficult to argue against the fact that a second-generation Christian was quoting all four Gospels less than 100 years after the life of Jesus. Within about 35 years of the authorship of John's Gospel, Papias was quoting John's words from a church in western Turkey.

"If I met with any one who had been a follower of the elders anywhere, I made it a point to inquire what were the declarations of the elders; what was said by Andrew, Peter, or Philip; what by Thomas, James, John, Matthew, or any other of the disciples of our Lord; what was said by Aristion and the presbyter John, disciples of the Lord. For I do not think that I derived so much benefit from books as from the living voice of those that are still surviving."

—**PAPIAS,** AS RECORDED BY THE EARLY CHURCH HISTORIAN EUSEBIUS

Papias said that he felt compelled to learn directly from those who had lived and served alongside the apostles of Jesus.

## Justin Martyr (100–165)

In the mid-second century, we find an additional extrabiblical source written by Justin Martyr, known as the best defender of Christianity during his era (A.D. 140). He considered all four Gospels to be accurate and communicated among the Roman culture of his time.

Justin Martyr quoted from the apostle John in Ephesus (modern-day Turkey) only a generation after the original text was written. This complements modern research that has dated a parchment scrap of John's Gospel to as early as A.D. 125.

"Christ also said 'Unless you are born again you will not enter into the kingdom of heaven.'"

—**JUSTIN MARTYR,** *I APOLOGIES* 61.4

## Polycarp (69–155)

Polycarp, a student of the apostle John, also quotes portions of Matthew, Mark, and Luke, referring to them as the very words of Jesus around A.D. 150.

## What the Early Church Fathers Said

Did the early church fathers believe Jesus was God? In addition to affirming the apostles' teaching on the subject, the following quotes show that the divinity of Jesus was established from the earliest times in Christianity:

- Clement (A.D. 95) called Jesus "the high priest of our offerings, the guardian and helper of our weaknesses....for he, being the radiance of his majesty, is as much superior to angels as the name he has inherited is more excellent."[17]

- 2 Clement (A.D. 180) noted that "we ought to think of Jesus Christ, as we do of God, as Judge of the living in the dead."

- Ignatius (A.D. 110) called Jesus "born and unborn, God in man" and "son of man and son of God."[18]

- Melito of Sardis (A.D. 160) in his Discourse on the Cross, said that Christians affirmed both the humanity and the divinity of Jesus side by side.

### Irenaeus (120–202)

Irenaeus, a student of Polycarp, quoted from 23 of the 27 New Testament books by A.D. 170, omitting only the shortest books, such as Philemon and 3 John.

### The Muratorian Fragment (c. 174)

By the last quarter of the second century, we discover two further Christian sources, including the Muratorian Fragment from A.D. 174, which lists Matthew, Mark, Luke, and John as the four Gospels. In total, this list includes 23 of the 27 New Testament books.

### Papyrus 45 (c. 200)

Finally, scholars have dated what they call Papyrus 45 at around A.D. 200. This remnant also mentions all four Gospels together and labels them as authentic writings by the followers of Jesus.

## Now What?

We can see from many sources that Jesus really did exist and that he actually performed at least some sort of newsworthy activities that resulted in his public execution. This can be confirmed historically even apart from the Bible, though the Gospels remain the most complete record of Jesus' activities as reported by those closest to him.

## What About the Missing Gospels?

Many books and documentaries today feature so-called missing gospels such as the *Gospel of Judas* and the *Gospel of Thomas*. Professors such as Harold Bloom have even claimed that the *Gospel of Thomas* is "[a gospel] that spares us the crucifixion, makes the resurrection unnecessary, and does not present us with a God named Jesus....If you turn to the *Gospel of Thomas*, you encounter a Jesus who is unsponsored and free."[19] How should we respond to these claims?

It is important to understand that these writings primarily come from a group of texts called the Nag Hammadi documents, which were found in 1945 and date from approximately 150 years after the New Testament documents were written. No scholar suggests that these were written by eyewitnesses or by those directly associated with Jesus or his apostles.

What are these mysterious Nag Hammadi documents? Upon investigation, we find that most of these texts consist of later works termed Gnostic gospels (*gnostic* is from the Greek word meaning "knowledge"):

> The Nag Hammadi Texts...are named after the place they were found on the west bank of the Nile. A library was found containing forty-five texts written in the Coptic language. These were written from the early second century to the fourth century A.D. Examples of texts included *The Gospel of Thomas, The Gospel of Philip, The Acts of Peter* and others. These texts were Gnostic in character and found in a library of Gnostic works....[20]

Gnosticism was a problem even in the first-century church. The claim that the Gnostic gospels are long-lost gospels can hardly withstand serious research. The church had known of these documents for centuries. Iraneaus (A.D. 130–200) and Tertullian (A.D. 160–225) mentioned these texts in their letters along with their rejection of them. These texts were never considered part of the inspired writings of the apostles.

But if Jesus was really that influential, wouldn't someone have painted a picture, constructed a monument, or named a school in his honor? At the very least, shouldn't his buddies have included some details in their writings that enable us to check on and confirm their accuracy? For instance, if Nazareth really was the hometown of Jesus, it would be good to know if it existed and if the historical evidence matches what the Bible says about Nazareth.

Our next chapter looks at the culture of Jesus' lifetime and examines what it can tell us about Jesus.

The World of Jesus:

# What Does His Culture Tell Us About Him?

**3**

*"To date, over 25,000 sites in biblical lands have been discovered, dating back to Old Testament times, which have established the accuracy of innumerable details in the Bible."*

—DR. RON RHODES[1]

We live in a postmodern, visually oriented culture. Four-year-olds play video games, teens build Web sites, and distance education via Internet and video technology has exploded information and learning beyond any other time in history.

The world of Jesus, in contrast, was a *premodern,* visually oriented culture. Though the people of Jesus' day lacked HDTV, video iPods, and DVD players in their minivans, they relied heavily on visual representations and word pictures to communicate ideas. The major reason for this style of life emerged from a low level of literacy. Historians estimate that as few as possibly only 10 percent of the people in the ancient Mediterranean world could read and write at a functional level. As a result, pictures, paintings, sculptures, and similar art forms flourished.

Early Christianity utilized such communication forms early on, using symbols such as a fish with the letters IXOYE, which was an acronym that meant "Jesus Christ God's Son is Savior." Another key symbol is the cross. Both symbols clearly point to Jesus' influence in the ancient world. In this chapter, we'll look at some archaeological evidence that confirms the accuracy of the New Testament accounts of Jesus' life.

During an interview on this topic, scholar Dr. Craig Evans made this comment about the geographical locations mentioned in the New Testament: "We can actually go to the place. It's a real place. It isn't some fairytale land somewhere. It isn't King Arthur and his round table. We can actually go someplace and say this is where it all happened. We've actually dug up the very pavement where Jesus walked. Things like that can be found."[2]

## According to the Experts

In an interview with distinguished Jewish archaeologist Dr. Gabriel Barkay, who recently was awarded the Jerusalem award for his archaeological research on ancient Jerusalem, I (John) asked him if he thought that the writers of the New Testament anchored their stories in real historical events. With confidence Barkay replied, "Yes, I do. I think that much of the evidence of the gospels mirrors a reality of the first century."[3]

In a prime-time television program I (John) filmed on location regarding the life of Jesus, we repeatedly found that Christian and non-Christian scholars alike confirmed the integrity of the New Testament's historical background. Dr. Magen Broshi, former curator of the Shrine of the Book, Israel's museum containing the Dead Sea Scrolls, said about the archaeological evidence found in the New Testament: "The setting is absolutely accurate. The geography is accurate. The mode of living...they couldn't have invented it, and they didn't have any need to invent anything."

Respected Jewish archaeologist Dr. Hillel Geva concurred with Broshi's words. He has worked on some of the most important archaeological excavations in Jerusalem since 1967 and is editor of the leading Hebrew journal on biblical archaeology in Israel. He notes that "the New Testament is a very authentic, historical book. No doubt there is history in it—real and authentic history in the book." In total, archaeologists have confirmed that Luke was so accurate that he cited facts about 32 countries, 54 cities, 9 islands, and several rulers without making one mistake.

## The Most Significant Finds

In the rest of this chapter, we'll take some time to highlight further details regarding a small number of these historical finds. For our conversation, we've selected seven of the most significant and relevant findings that help support the accuracy of the life of Jesus. Along the way we will point you to Web sites and other resources you can check out so you can see the specifics for yourself, if you prefer.

### *Jesus' Birthplace*

Bethlehem, Israel is the traditional birthplace of Jesus and therefore a holy site to Christians around the world. In 2001, I (John) traveled with a team to record a television series on location there. Bethlehem is now a bustling city, but it's still evident that there is a tremendous reverence for the fact this was the place of Jesus' earthly birth.

The traditional site of Jesus' birth was where the mother of the Roman emperor Constantine built the Church of the Nativity in the fourth century, about 300 years after the life of Christ. The site has been revered by Christians since Justin Martyr identified it as the historic site in the mid-second century.

Apparently the account of Jesus' birth in Bethlehem was so well known in the early second century that not only was the Roman emperor aware of the birthplace, but he was also aware of the specific location of the cave within Bethlehem. Early in the second century, Emperor Hadrian planted a grove of trees in honor of the god Adonis at the site as a deliberate insult to Christianity:

Both Jerome and Paulinus of Nola provide evidence that the cave in Bethlehem, under the present Church of the Nativity, was identified as the birthplace [of Jesus] before the time of [the Roman emperor] Hadrian—thus almost into the first century. Hadrian (117–38) marked the site by planting a grove of trees there in honor of the Roman god Adonis.[4]

What is the best explanation for the fact that knowledge of Jesus' birth as recorded in Matthew and Luke was so widespread in the early to mid-second century? There's little to support the allegation that Matthew and Luke were making up stories and were speaking only for highly isolated communities within the Christian world. It makes the most sense that Matthew and Luke recorded old, widely accepted traditions that were considered credible by the earliest Christians, including Jesus' relatives.[5]

### They Said It:

"The tradition of a birth site like Bethlehem is actually strengthened by the fact that the earliest record that we have of the tradition of Jesus' birthplace goes back to Justin Martyr, who, 15–20 years after Bethlehem was totally destroyed by Roman armies, said that the pilgrims came to visit a cave. We go there today. It's at the top of a hill, which is exactly where a patriarchal home would be built—on top of a hill. Patriarchal homes are kept for many genera-tions, and kept within the family. So the tradition of Jesus' birthplace there in the middle of the second century is actually extremely close to the time when those homes were still in existence in Bethlehem. So knowing that Jesus was born there, that his family's patriarchal home would have persisted there until their destruction around A.D. 137, and then just 15 or 20 years later Justin Martyr states that's where people commemorated his birth, actually brings it into the category of probably being the place where Jesus was born."

—DR. D.S. PFANN, DIRECTOR OF THE JERUSALEM SCHOOL FOR THE STUDY
OF EARLY CHRISTIANITY AND OF THE NAZARETH VILLAGE[6]

According to Dr. Darrell Bock, research professor of New Tes-tament at Dallas Theological Seminary, "I think He was born in Bethlehem. In fact, again, let's take the alternative. What evidence is there that He was born in Nazareth? And my response would be,

'Silence.' There is none."[7] Dr. D.S. Pfann, a professor who lives in Israel, notes that "there's only one tradition concerning Jesus' birth-place, and that's Bethlehem."[8]

## Jesus' Hometown

Nazareth is not mentioned in the Old Testament or any other ancient Jewish sources. However, in 1961, an early Hebrew inscrip-tion was found in Caesarea that mentions Nazareth. In Jesus' day, Nazareth would have had a population of about 500. This matches the New Testament picture that portrayed Nazareth as an obscure, unnoteworthy village. In the Gospel of John, people who hear of Jesus of Nazareth ask themselves, "Can any good thing come out of Nazareth?"[9]

---

### Wasn't Jesus an Only Child?

In contrast with the Catholic tradition of Immaculate Conception, Matthew specifically wrote that Jesus had brothers and sisters:

> When Jesus had finished these parables, he moved on from there. Coming to his hometown, he began teaching the people in their syna-gogue, and they were amazed. "Where did this man get this wisdom and these miraculous powers?" they asked. "Isn't this the carpen-ter's son? Isn't his mother's name Mary, and aren't his brothers James, Joseph, Simon and Judas? Aren't all his sisters with us? Where then did this man get all these things?"
>
> —MATTHEW 13:53-56

How do Catholic theologians handle this quote? Because of prior theolog-ical assumptions about Mary the mother of Jesus, they usually suggest that "brothers" and "sisters" here mean cousins or other relatives. However, a straightforward reading seems to clearly indicate that the young Jesus was only one of many siblings.

---

According to the accounts written by Jesus' friends, Nazareth was the home of his mother Mary and of Joseph,[10] the site of the angelic announcement to Mary that she would give birth to the Savior, and the town where Jesus grew up.[11]

Respected Jewish archaeologist Dr. Magen Broshi, in an

on-location interview regarding the early life of Jesus, said that
the New Testament's information about Jesus' hometown "fits very
well of what we know about first-century Palestine. It fits very well
because it gives us a good picture of what was happening here, and
archaeology can prove it."[12]

---

"[Joseph] went and lived in a town called Nazareth. So was fulfilled what was
said through the prophets: '[Jesus] will be called a Nazarene.' "[13]

—MATTHEW 2:23

---

*Jacob's Well*

In John 4, we encounter Jesus in a deeply spiritual conversation
with a Samaritan woman. This event took place at a location called
Jacob's Well. Is this a place we could visit today?

The site still exists, though the well itself is now usually quite
dry. It is at the entrance to the valley between Ebal and Gerizim,
about two miles southeast of Shechem. The well is about nine feet
in diameter and about 75 feet deep, though in ancient times it was
no doubt much deeper, probably twice as deep. The digging of such
a well must have been very time-consuming and costly.

One expert said this about the location:

> Unfortunately, the well of Jacob has not escaped that mis-
> placed religious worship of holy sites. A series of buildings
> of various styles, and of different ages, have cumbered the
> ground, choked up the well, and disfigured the natural
> beauty and simplicity of the spot. At present the rubbish
> in the well has been cleared out, but there is still a domed
> structure over it, and you gaze down the shaft cut in the
> living rock and see at a depth of 70 feet the surface of the
> water glimmering with a pale blue light in the darkness,
> while you notice how the limestone blocks that form its
> curb have been worn smooth, or else furrowed by the ropes
> of centuries.[14]

It is at this well that the apostle John, one of Jesus' closest friends, writes in John chapter 4 about Jesus as God's Son. In this account, we read about how Jesus transitions the conversation with the Samaritan woman from physical water to the water of life (Jesus himself). He notes the woman's marital background as if he were all-knowing, and he convinces the woman he is a prophet. By the end of their discussion together, she abandons her water jug, heads back to the village, and gathers other people, saying, "Come, see a man who told me everything I ever did. Could this be the Christ?"[15]

## Why the Racial Conflict?

In addition to unresolved conflicts due to earlier generations of intermarriage between the Jews and Samaritans, which the Jews believed made their people unclean, there were many worldview differences between the Jews and Samaritans. Dr. Hall Harris notes:

> There was *theological opposition* between the Samaritans and the Jews because the former refused to worship in Jerusalem. After the exile the Samaritans put obstacles in the way of the Jewish restoration of Jerusalem, and in the second century B.C. the Samaritans helped the Syrians in their wars against the Jews. In 128 B.C. the Jewish high priest retaliated and burned the Samaritan temple on Mount Gerazim.[16]

In the first century, Samaritans and Jews even considered sharing a cup of water as an unclean religious act, something Jesus was not afraid to do to draw in the woman's interest in John 4.

Jesus stayed two more days in the area, and as a result, many of the villagers came to believe in him as the Messiah. For this to happen in a Samaritan village—a group culturally hostile with Jews in their time—indicates that a monumental transformation had taken place. For John's original audience, this would have been considered nothing less than a miracle. Samaritans believing in a carpenter Jew as the coming Messiah? According to John, this was clear evidence that Jesus was God's Son.

---

### Where Is Jacob's Well?

Shechem is found in modern Nablus, a contraction for Neopolis, the name given to it by the Roman emperor Vespasian. It lies about a mile and a half up the valley on its southern slope, and on the north of Gerizim, which rises about 1,100 feet above it, and is about 34 miles north of Jerusalem. It has about 10,000 inhabitants, of whom about 160 are Samaritans and 100 Jews, the rest being Christians and Mohammedans.[17] You can still tour the area today through services such as those provided through www.shechem.org.

---

### *The Synagogue in Capernaum*

The Jewish synagogue in Capernaum lies on the shore of the Sea of Galilee in Israel. It was in this town that Jesus taught "as one who had authority, not as the teachers of the law."[18] The synagogue at Capernaum is where Jesus was confronted by a demon-possessed man while teaching,[19] where Jesus healed the servant of the centurion,[20] and where Jesus gave his message on the bread of life.[21] If this synagogue could be found, it would offer another cultural affirmation of the life of Jesus and the reliability of his friends' statements about him.

---

### A Franciscan Indiana Jones?

Franciscan monks have been responsible for most of the archaeological research on the synagogue in Capernaum. Beginning in 1969, excavations revealed the remains of a synagogue foundation dating to the time of Jesus. This was found below the ancient ruins of a still-standing fourth-century structure. Several pictures and scholarly articles on these excavations have been placed on the Internet.[22]

---

Fortunately, archaeologists have rediscovered this synagogue. The excavators observe that "among today's remains of Capernaum lies a fourth-century synagogue of white limestone. The foundation of this synagogue is constructed of black basaltic stone, probably dating to the first-century synagogue built by the Roman centurion who was stationed in Capernaum in Luke 7:5."[23] In other words, the synagogue has been accurately noted as existing during the lifetime of Jesus. While this does not prove that Jesus is God's Son or even healed anyone, it does show that what his friends said about him fits within what is known by archaeologists of his contemporary surroundings and culture.

---

## Has the Tomb of Lazarus "Come Forth"?

The first catacomb found near Bethany (the town where Lazarus lived) was investigated by renowned French archaeologist Charles Clermont-Ganneau. The other, a large burial cemetery unearthed near the modern Dominus Flevit Chapel, was excavated by Italian scholar P. Bagatti.

Both archaeologists found evidence clearly dating the two catacombs to the first century A.D., with the latter finding coins minted by Governor Varius Gratus at the turn of the millenium (up to A.D.15/16). Evidence in both catacombs indicated their use for burial until the middle part of the first century A.D., several years before the New Testament was written.

The first catacomb was a family tomb investigated by archaeologist Clermont-Ganneau on the Mount of Olives near the ancient town of Bethany. Clermont-Ganneau was surprised to find names that corresponded with names in the New Testament. Even more interesting were the signs of the cross etched on several of the ossuaries (stone coffins).

As Claremont-Ganneau further investigated the tomb, he found inscriptions, including the names *Eleazar* (Lazarus), *Martha* and *Mary* on three different coffins.

—**JEAN GILMAN**, *JERUSALEM CHRISTIAN REVIEW*[24]

---

### The Tomb of Lazarus

One of the most remarkable miracles communicated from the lifetime of Jesus was his raising of Lazarus from the dead four days after Lazarus died. In contrast with modern skeptics, multiple ancient Christian writings indicate that the tomb in which Lazarus was buried and later raised from continued to be visited by later generations of people. For instance:

- The early church historian Eusebius, writing around A.D. 330, noted that the place of Lazarus was still known.

- In A.D. 333, a guide pointed out to the Pilgrim of Bordeaux the "crypt" where Lazarus had been laid to rest.

- In A.D. 390, St. Jerome mentioned a church built near the "place of Lazarus."

Again, such archaeological finds do not prove that Jesus raised Lazarus from the dead, but they do indicate that Jesus was a literal, historical figure who was active in a particular area at the time his friends said he lived. Unlike many religions, in which the leaders are entirely mythical or nonphysical in nature, Jesus was known as a spiritual leader who lived and taught among the common people of his day. For those who examine the information, the historical evidence from Christian, Jewish, and Greco-Roman sources all record that Jesus healed the sick, sent away demons, and even raised Lazarus from the dead.

## Lazarus in Art

"Judging by the number of surviving reproductions, the raising of Lazarus made a deeper impression on early Christian artists than almost any other New Testament periscope [story]. Art historians have catalogued more than 55 paintings of Lazarus's resurrection in the third- and fourth-century Roman catacombs."

—NOTED IN *BIBLICAL ARCHAEOLOGY REVIEW*[25]

### Pilate's Stone

It wasn't long ago when many scholars were questioning the actual existence of a Roman governor with the name Pontius Pilate, the procurator who ordered Jesus' crucifixion. In June 1961, Italian archaeologists led by Dr. Frova were excavating an ancient Roman amphitheatre near Caesarea on the Sea and uncovered an interesting limestone block. On the face of this block is a monumental inscription that is part of a larger dedication to Tiberius Caesar, which clearly says that it was from "Pontius Pilate, Prefect of Judea."[26] The inscription is as follows:

*TIBERIEUM,*

[PON]*TIUS*

[PRAEF]*ECTUS IUDA*[EAE]

The only written information regarding Pontius Pilate outside of the New Testament comes from two Jewish writers: Josephus and Philo of Alexandria. Both writers noted that at one time, Pilate had placed golden shields on the walls of his palace on Mount Zion bearing inscriptions of the names of various gods. Tiberius Caesar had to personally order the removal of the shields. Another time, Pilate used temple revenues to build his aqueduct (water lines). There is another incident only recorded in the Bible where Pilate ordered the slaughter of certain Galileans (Luke 13:1) who had supposedly been offering sacrifices in the temple.[27]

---

"Philo tells us (*Legatio ad Caium,* xxxviii) that on another occasion he dedicated some gilt shields in the palace of Herod in honor of the emperor. On these shields there was no representation of any forbidden thing, but simply an inscription of the name of the donor and of him in whose honor they were set up. The Jews petitioned him to have them removed; when he refused, they appealed to Tiberius, who sent an order that they should be removed to Caesarea."

—FROM *INTERNATIONAL STANDARD BIBLE ENCYCLOPAEDIA*

---

When the Mel Gibson film *The Passion of the Christ* released in 2004, my (John's) friend Dr. Darrell Bock was interviewed on ABC with Diane Sawyer regarding his thoughts on the movie's accuracy. Shortly afterward, I interviewed Darrell for my show as well, and asked for his extended thoughts on the film's portrayal of Pilate and the death of Jesus.

His words match what we see in this archaeological find

concerning Pilate. "I think this is the most accurate film that we've had yet of Jesus' final hours. It doesn't step back from the violence of crucifixion....It also gets into the tensions of first-century politics in an effective way; particularly, the complexity of Jesus' relationship to the Jewish leadership as well as the complexity of the Jewish relationship to Pilate and to Rome. And it does so in a way that shows the tensions of first-century politics and the inconsistencies in some of the relationships as they waffle and waver to figure out exactly how to deal with what they perceive to be a difficult situation."[28]

## Did You Know...?

Archaeologists have found a few bronze coins that were struck from A.D. 29–32 by Pontius Pilate.[29]

### The Tomb of Jesus

Without a doubt, the most important physical location related to Jesus is his tomb. Originally belonging to the affluent Joseph of Arimathea, the Gospel writers indicate that Jesus' body was enclosed inside a rock-hewn cave before nightfall on Friday and guarded by a team of Roman soldiers. Three days later the tomb was empty, a fact undisputed by Jewish and Roman leaders. Enemies argued that Jesus' followers stole the body. His followers believed Jesus died, was honorably buried by Joseph of Arimathea, and then physically rose from the dead and appeared to them individually and in groups.

### How Does this Help Me?

When asked about the importance of archaeology in the life of Jesus, Dr. Craig Evans, a New Testament professor who has lectured at Cambridge, Durham, Oxford, and conferences around the world, shared in an interview that "archaeology doesn't prove that Jesus was really God's Son. But what it does is show that there is a historical foundation on which confessions of faith make perfectly good sense."[30]

Archaeological evidence helps us better understand what Jesus' friends wrote about him in the Bible. If the locations mentioned by Jesus' friends are historically reliable, and they are places we can still visit today, then what remains is to make a decision as to whether Jesus' supernatural acts, such as his claim to be God and his resurrection from the dead, are also real parts of history. If so, then we are faced with someone who has called for us to change our lives to follow and serve him. In his messages, Jesus invited people to forgiveness for their sins, strength for living life today, and a hope-filled afterlife.

Sound good? Of course, but how do we know if these teachings were passed down faithfully? How reliable are the sources we have today, and how do we know whether they can be trusted? That's the focus of our next chapter.

# How Reliable Are the Manuscripts We Have Today?

**4**

*"The notion that God's only son came to this planet to offer his life as a sacrifice for the sins of the world and that God could not forgive us without that having happened, and that we are saved by believing this story, is simply incredible....Taken literally, it is a profound obstacle to accepting the Christian message. To many people it simply makes no sense."*

—MARCUS BORG, IN *MEETING JESUS AGAIN FOR THE FIRST TIME*[1]

**M**ost scholars hold that Jesus taught from the late 20s to the early 30s. He chose 12 apostles to follow him for a three-year period, then spread his message. The New Testament books were based on a connection with the 12 apostles and the teachings of Jesus through the following nine sources:

- **Two apostles**, Matthew and John, wrote Gospels. John also wrote three letters and the book of Revelation.

- **Peter** authored two letters and was the source for **Mark**'s Gospel.

- **Luke** based his Gospel on the eyewitness testimonies

of the apostles. He was also a traveling companion of the apostle Paul. Paul later quotes Luke's Gospel as Scripture in 1 Timothy 5:18.

- **James and Jude** were human brothers of Jesus. James did not believe in Jesus until after Jesus' resurrection. James later became bishop of the Jerusalem church and wrote the New Testament book of James. Jude believed after the resurrection as well, writing the book that bears his name.

- **The author of Hebrews** was well known to his recipients but not to everyone in the church. This delayed the book's acceptance to some. Some claim the author was Barnabas, a fellow missionary with Paul. Others believe Apollos wrote it during his early years with Paul in Corinth. Either way, both had direct contact with an apostle.

- **Paul** authored 13 of the 27 New Testament books and was recognized as authoritative by Peter.[2]

Nine individuals wrote the 27 books received by the churches and recognized as scripture. All were written and received by A.D. 95, with most books written within 40 years after the events of Jesus' life. Within approximately one generation of the New Testament's completion, every book had been cited by a church father.[3] And in A.D. 367, the church leader Athanasius compiled a list of these 27 books, which, by this time, church leaders across the Roman Empire had accepted as authoritative.[4]

## Then and Now

Today's technologies allow for materials to be duplicated at a level of extreme accuracy. For instance, when copies of *USA Today* are produced and distributed worldwide, each copy is exactly alike for the day. Automated systems of computers and printers provide a miniscule level of error even on the scale of millions of copies.

Such was not the case during the lifetime of Jesus. There was no local copier shop at which Jesus could reproduce his speech outlines or duplicate the latest press releases. Instead, every copy of every document required line-by-line, word-by-word hand copying. An entire industry of professional scribes existed in those days specifically for the purpose of writing dictation and duplicating important works for those who could afford such services.

It is because of this primitive system of transmission that some have argued that the New Testament writings we have today cannot be trusted. They reason that after centuries of hand copying, surely substantial changes have occurred as a result of scribal inaccuracies. One recent New York bestseller provocatively titled *Misquoting Jesus* suggests this:

> In some instances, the very meaning of the text is at stake, depending on how one resolves a textual problem: Was Jesus an angry man [Mark 1.41]? Was he completely distraught in the face of death [Heb 2.8–9]? Did he tell his disciples that they could drink poison without being harmed [Mark 16.9–20]? Did he let an adulteress off the hook with nothing but a mild warning [John 7.53–8.11]? Is the doctrine of the Trinity explicitly taught in the New Testament [1 John 5.7–8]? Is Jesus actually called "the unique God" there [John 1.18]? Does the New Testament indicate that even the Son of God himself does not know when the end will come [Matt 24.36]? The questions go on and on, and all of them are related to how one resolves difficulties in the manuscript tradition as it has come down to us.[5]

It's one thing to make such claims against the writings concerning Jesus. It's quite another to show it.

When we talk about the accuracy of the New Testament's transmission, what we really want to know is if *what was written then is what we have now*. We don't really care that much if someone accidentally put an extra *t* on the end of a word or duplicated a letter.

We're concerned whether the writings left by those who spent time with Jesus during the first century are the same writings available for our study today.

In the twentieth century, much debate took place over the manuscript evidence for the reliability of the New Testament books. In *The Bible and Archaeology,* Sir Frederic G. Kenyon, former director and principal librarian of the British Museum, stated:

> The interval, then, between the dates of original composition and the earliest extant evidence becomes so small as to be in fact negligible, and the last foundation for any doubt that the Scriptures have come down to us substantially as they were written has now been removed. Both the authenticity and the general integrity of the books of the New Testament may be regarded as finally established.[6]

## War of the Words

B.F. Westcott and F.J.A. Hort, the editors of *The New Testament in Original Greek,* commented: "If comparative trivialities such as changes of order, the insertion or omission of the article with proper names, and the like are set aside, the works in our opinion still subject to doubt can hardly amount to more than a thousandth part of the whole New Testament."[7]

How do we approach this issue of the New Testament's integrity? Scholars have discussed these issues at length for generations. What further can we say about it?

When it comes to conversing on this matter, it seems to make the most sense to take a look at the two key elements involved in the process—the copyists and the copies.

## The Copyists: Who's Responsible for This?

In the beginning, faithful church leaders with literacy skills promptly began hand-copying the books that comprise the New

Testament. This function was carried on heavily by monastics in the second and early third centuries. Within the first few centuries of the church, portions of the New Testament were translated into other languages, including Latin, Aramaic, Armenian, Georgian, Ethiopic, Gothic, and Slavonic.

Imagine the following scenario: You are a teacher standing in front of a room of 50 ten-year-old children. In your hand are 50 copies of Abraham Lincoln's Gettysburg Address. The spelling and punctuation of your 50 copies are absolutely perfect and uniform. You announce to the children, "Today's assignment is to copy this speech, word for word." All the students pull out their pencils, complete the task, and turn in their papers. Then you shred your original copies, and using the students' copies, you attempt to reconstruct the original.

In this situation, what would help you the most in reconstructing the original? One copy? Ten copies? Fifty? The answer is, The more, the merrier. Why? Because you can identify *consistency*. With 50 copies in hand, you could test any out-of-place words or punctuations against 49 other copies.

Let's switch from imagination to the classics of literature. How many early copies exist of the writings of Aristotle? Forty-nine. What about Plato? Seven. Based on even these small numbers, classical scholars today would say we can be pretty certain we have what Plato originally said. Are these isolated cases? Let's check out a few more. The great writer Sophocles? We have 193 copies. Thucydides? Eight. Catullus, the great ancient poet? Three. Lucretius? Only two.

The second-best attested book from ancient history is Homer's *The Iliad*. How many early copies remain of this work? There are 643. From the perspective of classical scholars, this number of copies is considered outstanding.

Compare these statistics with the numbers of early copies we have of the New Testament documents. Many have claimed today's New Testament documents are unreliable, so how do they compare with Plato or Homer? Over *24,633 manuscripts,* portions or entire manuscripts of the New Testament, exist today! Dr. Bruce Metzger, in his groundbreaking book *The Text of the New Testament,* wrote, "The works of several ancient authors are preserved to us by the thinnest possible thread of transmission. In contrast with these figures of the classics, the textual critic of the New Testament is embarrassed by the wealth of his material."[8]

---

### What the Experts Say:

- The late Dr. William F. Albright observed that "only modern scholars who lack both historical method and perspective can spin such a web of speculation as that with which the critics have surrounded the gospel tradition."

- F.F. Bruce at Manchester University, Rylands Professor of Biblical Criticism and Exegesis, said, "There is no body of ancient literature in the world which enjoys such a wealth of good textual attestation as the New Testament."

- Frederick Kenyon, former librarian at the British Museum, wrote, "Both the authenticity and the general integrity of the books of the New Testament may be regarded as finally established."[9]

---

How should we understand this abundance of documentation regarding the New Testament books? While the staggering numbers of manuscripts does not necessarily prove that what the Bible says is true, it does allow us to test whether the texts have been accurately transmitted over the past 2,000 years. Any genuine dispute with what the text *says* requires a challenge against what thousands of ancient copies have recorded for centuries. Therefore, a more informed approach is to seek the truth of what those words actually *claim.*

While the abundance of early copies of the New Testament is a good thing, still, minor errors did show up in some copies. That is why, in A.D. 382, Pope Damasus called upon the early church theologian Jerome to make an official Latin version that would remedy the minor discrepancies between the existing translations and would serve as a standard reference for future copies. Jerome's work was based on his careful study of numerous Greek manuscripts, and his work became the standard Bible for the Latin-speaking world until the Protestant Reformation—for the next 1,000 years!

## Reasons for Copyists' Errors:

There were a number of reasons that variant copies came about; the vast majority of them were unintentional. They included:

1. **Eye Skips:** These included misreadings that resulted in omissions, repetitions, and transpositions of letters, words, and even entire lines.

2. **Similar Endings or Beginnings:** When the confusion is due to similar endings on two words or lines such that the intervening words end up being omitted, the error is termed *homoeoteleuton* (similar ending). When the omission is due to similar beginnings, it is termed *homoeoarcton*.

3. **Mishearing:** If a book was being dictated it would be inevitable that a scribe might mishear what was said. Such a situation appears to have arisen in Romans 5:1—"we have peace" and "let us have peace"—both of which sound the same in the original Greek text.

4. **Poor Judgment:** A copyist might misinterpret the abbreviations that were often used in manuscripts. This was especially true with the name of Jesus, where there are sometimes manuscript variations between *Jesus, Jesus Christ, Christ,* and *Christ Jesus.*

5. **Added Instructions:** Liturgical instructions also may have been added in some cases, where a "footnote" became part of a later manuscript.

6. **Deliberate Changes:** While skeptics argue many such changes, those that have been identified clearly stand out due to the massive number of correct copies that are available for comparison. In other words, if a change was intentionally made, the other copies that had not been changed would show which one was inaccurate.

By the time of the Renaissance, the Greek scholar Erasmus produced an edited Greek New Testament based on his study of available Greek manuscripts. While not perfect, its popularity grew with the technology of the printing press. With the revolution of the Protestant Reformation, the New Testament began to again flourish in new languages, such as German (via Luther's New Testament in 1522) and English (via Wycliffe in 1380 and Tyndale's efforts in 1526). Throughout the English-speaking world, several translations evolved, with the King James Version (1611) enjoying the greatest popularity until the twentieth century.

### 150,000 Variants?

Some have estimated there are as many as over 150,000 differences among the numerous copies of the New Testament.[10] How can anyone really believe we can figure out what the original wording of these texts might have been?

The answer lies in a correct understanding of *what kinds* of differences exist. Suppose we have five manuscript copies of an original document that no longer exists. Each copy is different as follows:

Manuscript #1: Jesus Christ is the Savior of the whole worl.
Manuscript #2: Christ Jesus is the Savior of the whole world.
Manuscript #3: Jesus Christ s the Savior of the whole world.
Manuscript #4: Jesus Christ is th Savior of the whle world.
Manuscript #5: Jesus Christ is the Savor of the whole wrld.

Could we figure out what the original document most likely said? Unless the apostles wrote in slang or with typos, then we would agree this is not an impossible challenge. Conservative scholars comment that over 99 percent of such "variants" are of this nature.[11]

## The Copies: What Are the Earliest Writings?

There are some who say, "There are no original copies of the New Testament remaining. We have no idea what was really written."

Such accusations are often made against the Bible's integrity, and it is true that no original New Testament documents have survived to this day (or yet been found). But we have thousands of early manuscripts and fragments that come from as early as A.D. 125, only one generation removed from the originals. Clement, writing in A.D. 95, quotes from several New Testament books, clearly indicating the existence of those writings prior to this date. Some scholars have even redated some of the early fragments to possible first-century dates, suggesting *same-generation* copies of the gospels.[12]

"How good are these documents? If the New Testament documents were written by drunken monks in the tenth century, Christianity is in deep trouble. But they weren't. They were written by eyewitnesses of the events themselves, or by associates of eyewitnesses."

—DR. JOHN WARWICK MONTGOMERY[13]

The entire Bible, Old and New Testament, is certainly unique among all the books of the world. Its contents were written by 40 authors over a period of 1,500 years. To find the Bible in agreement in its teachings demands much more than a human explanation. Followers of Jesus believe such a collection of writings can only be explained through God's supernatural intervention.

## Now What?

So we've taken some time to share what Jesus' friends said about him. We've discovered that the majority of writings by other authors during the Jesus Generation mentioned his impact. The historical references in the Gospel fit the landscape of Jesus' culture. Textual criticism teaches us that these earliest writings about Jesus have been handed down to us intact. What does all this mean for us *now?*

In seeking to understand the big deal about Jesus, we're beginning to grasp the enormous number of relationships and circumstances that point to Jesus as really coming back to life and being God's son. But does the fact Jesus' *friends* claimed that he said he was divine mean that Jesus *himself* thought and said he was God? This question will guide us through part two of our time together as we consider who Jesus actually claimed to be.

**Part Two:** | # Who Did Jesus Claim to Be?

*"Jesus never claimed to be God."*

*"Jesus might have been a real person, but that didn't mean he was deity."*

*"Wasn't Jesus 'made' divine centuries later?"*

*"He was a great religious leader."*

*"I don't think Jesus really thought he was God's Son. Maybe it was just symbolic."*

Everyone has their own view of who Jesus is today. Jesus has gone "pop" in our culture—he is found on T-shirts and on greeting cards. Films such as *The Passion of the Christ* and *The Nativity* have brought Jesus to the big screen, while politicians key in on evangelical voters during the election season. Over 90 percent of Americans believe in the existence of a higher power. They just can't seem to agree on what that power is.

Our conversation takes a turn in this section from the testimonies left by the friends and world of Jesus to the claims Jesus made about himself and the actions that, according to him, backed those claims. To communicate it another way, who did Jesus really think he was? A healer? A preacher? A spiritual guru? Was he sincere but misguided? Was he just a well-meaning nice guy? Or was he something more?

In case you're wondering if we're going to just knock down various theories about Jesus with a bunch of statistics and quotes, you may be surprised to find that is not the case. Instead, we intend primarily to peer directly into the Bible itself and let its words guide us through four major areas of discussion.

First, we'll investigate what the New Testament says about the miracles of Jesus. Did he really perform supernatural acts? What evidence outside of the Bible confirms this possibility?

Second, we'll look at what Jesus said about himself. What did *he* think about who he was? How would his audience have understood his teachings?

Then our attention will focus on the personality of Jesus as portrayed in the four Gospels. Were the activities and habits of Jesus similar to those of someone we would call mentally challenged? Did he appear to intentionally deceive his friends and the crowds who followed him? Was he just another great spiritual leader? Or was he God in human form?

Fourth, we'll tackle the complex world of Bible prophecies related to Jesus. Did he really fulfill the Old Testament prophecies about the coming Messiah? Did his followers "force" the connections between Jesus and the ancient prophets? How easy would it have been to really fulfill such predictions? Were the fulfillments mere coincidences or something more?

So grab another cup of coffee and dive in with us as we enter the Gospels for a deeper look at one of history's most intriguing questions: Who did Jesus claim to be?

The Miracles of Jesus:

# Did He Really Perform Super-natural Acts?

**5**

*"Despite the difficulty which miracles pose for the modern mind, on historical grounds it is virtually indisputable that Jesus was a healer and exorcist."*

—MARCUS BORG, IN *JESUS, A NEW VISION*[1]

*"I find it quite improbable that such order came out of chaos. There has to be some organizing principle. God to me is a mystery, but [he] is the explanation of the miracle of existence, and why there is something instead of nothing."*

—ALLAN SANDAGE, 1991 WINNER OF THE CRAFOORD PRIZE IN ASTRONOMY[2]

**W**hich is it? Did Jesus perform miracles or not? How can we *know* Jesus actually performed miracles? What do today's scholars believe?

In an interview for *The John Ankerberg Show,* Oxford scholar Dr. N.T. Wright stated, "It's one of the remarkable games of contemporary history on Jesus, that a majority of current Jesus scholars, including many who are not Christian believers, agree that Jesus *did* do remarkable healings. That is the main explanation for why he attracted crowds and drew so many followers. It wasn't just that his teaching was exciting, though it was. They came because things were happening. A great aunt who had been sick for 50 years: 'Bring her and Jesus will heal her.' That draws the crowds and would do so today if it were to happen."[3]

Yet there are those who continue to dispute that Jesus performed miracles. Why? Dr. William Lane Craig suggested in our discussion that "members of the Jesus Seminar who are skeptical in their approach to the New Testament have made many of their presuppositions abundantly clear....Their number one pillar of scholarly investigation of the historical Jesus is the presupposition of naturalism—that miracles do not happen."

But the evidence makes such a presupposition difficult to hold with integrity. According to Dr. Gary Habermas, "If there is a Creator, a Designer of the universe, who has brought it into being, if such a being exists, then clearly he could intervene in the course of history and perform miraculous acts. It seems to me that *we have to be open to the possibility of miracles.*"

## Supernatural Scholarship

According to Habermas, "Most scholars, the vast majority today, would say that Jesus did at least the healing miracles and the exorcisms. Then they add that he did something *like* these but they weren't truly supernatural. So now the question is, What data do we have for the supernaturalness of Jesus' miracles? I'd say again, you're looking at a lot of reasons here that are very respectful."

*How Do We Know?*

Habermas states, "The miracles of Jesus are attested in all the gospel strata. They're in Mark, they're in special Matthew [the parts of Matthew unique to only that Gospel], they're in special Luke, they're in John, and they're in the source, what the scholars call *Q*. What you have in Matthew and Luke, that's not in Mark. Miracles are reported in all five levels, and multiple attestation counts a lot."

Jewish secular professor Dr. Amy-Jill Levine suggested in an interview that "I do think Jesus was a miracle worker, along with several other miracle workers we have both in Jewish sources and in pagan sources. Would his miracle-working have been attributed to God? Certainly by some, but as we have even seen in the Gospels, others would have said, 'Oh, yes, we agree he did miracles, but he does them by the power of Satan.' *The miracle working itself is unquestioned*" (emphasis added).

### What Is Q?

Q is a hypothetical source document for the books of Matthew, Mark, and Luke, and is sometimes called the "sayings Gospel" because it is thought to consist mainly of Jesus' speeches, with little or no narrative. Q is one component of the theory of Markan priority, which holds that Mark was the first Gospel, and that Matthew and Luke were written with Mark as one source and Q as another.[4]

### Why the Change?

I (John) asked Dr. Craig Evans what reasons have compelled so many non-Christian scholars to admit Jesus must have performed miracles. He observed, "I can remember, as a university student, when the idea of any kind of miracle story was laughed at. That has changed in the past thirty years. You can see it in popular culture. You can see it in the popular television program *Star Trek*. Mr. Spock wants to be a machine, right? He wants to be *scientific*. Science can solve everything. In the new version of it, you have a machine who wants to be a human. You have characters who want to be in touch with the inner spirit and channel and do all kinds of strange things. That show reflects the change that has taken place.

"In science, there's the recognition 'Hey, we don't have a closed universe any more. We have to be open. We're not real sure about our origins anymore. Maybe there is something beyond the physical universe. Maybe there *is* a God. Maybe miracles *do* occur.' That's a big change."

"No other religion has any miracle that can be compared to the resurrection of Jesus Christ in its grandeur or its testimony."

—DR. NORMAN GEISLER[5]

## What About the Skeptics?

Still, there are some scholars and historians who refuse to admit Jesus performed miracles. Dr. Craig identified some examples. "Members, for example, of the Jesus Seminar, who are skeptical in their approach to the New Testament, have made many of their presuppositions abundantly clear. They've listed them, for example, in the introduction to their edition of the so-called *Five Gospels*." One of these presuppositions, as we read earlier, is that miracles do not happen.

Yet according to Dr. N.T. Wright, "My history makes me say, 'Hey, put that stuff on hold for a moment.' Just supposing Jesus of Nazareth really did rise from the dead. Don't start by saying, 'Did he walk on water?' Don't start by saying, 'Was he born of a virgin?' If you start with those questions, you go round and round in circles and you never get anywhere. Start by saying, 'How do you explain the rise of early Christianity?' If it comes back and says, 'It was Jesus' resurrection,' then you're going to have to hold your mind open to the fact that in the world, as Shakespeare said, '[There are] more things in heaven and earth than are dreamed of in your philosophy.'"

## The Predetermined Bias of Naturalism

But what can be said to the person who believes in the naturalistic theory that miracles *never* happen, and therefore all history must be investigated from this assumption? Dr. William Lane Craig says, "Since the story of the Gospels is, from start to finish, a story of miracles—the virgin birth, the incarnation, the exorcisms, the healings, the clairvoyant knowledge of the future, prophecy, the resurrection of Jesus—anyone who comes to the text with that presupposition is, of course, going to be forced to discount vast sections of the text as being unhistorical. But it's important to see that this conclusion is not based on the evidence. It's built into the *presupposition*. If you come to the Gospels with the presupposition of naturalism, then of course what you wind up with will be a purely human Jesus. So the issue there isn't one of evidence; the issue there is one of presuppositions. What is the justification for this presupposition of naturalism?"

What needs to be noted is that the historical evidence itself indicates the naturalistic assumption that miracles never happen is not true. What is this evidence? It's the fact that secular writers in history described Jesus as a miracle worker. These writers had no reason to argue otherwise. Unless Jesus was actually known to them through their sources as a miracle worker, they had no reason for describing him as such. We discussed numerous examples of this in chapter 2, including non-Christian sources such as Josephus, the Jewish rabbis in the Talmud, and the pagan philosopher Celsus—all of whom cited Jesus as a miracle worker.

Dr. Ben Witherington confirmed these historical facts. "What's interesting is that it's not just the New Testament that claims Jesus was a miracle worker. Later Jewish traditions, which rejected that Jesus was the Messiah, also attest that Jesus did miracles. It is also true that some of the later Greco-Roman sources also attest that Jesus was a miracle worker. And then, of course, we have the famous testimony of Josephus to the same effect. Do we have credible testimonies that Jesus did miracles? I think we do have some of those. But if you have presuppositions that miracles don't happen, then none of that's good enough."

In other words, those who refuse to look at the evidence because of their unproven naturalistic theory that miracles never happen cannot deal honestly with the historical evidence.

According to Dr. Darrell Bock, "If you come to the text and you believe miracles can't happen, you have a dilemma on your hands. You read these texts about Jesus multiplying the loaves or you read these texts about Jesus healing the blind, and you have to come up with some kind of explanation for what happened. In fact, the healing of the blind is an interesting one because in the Old Testament, blind people didn't get healed. No one did that miracle. And that's not one you can very easily fake."

Dr. William Lane Craig remarked, "It would be bad methodology to simply dismiss the miracles in advance before even looking at the evidence that they might have actually occurred. Otherwise, we could be ruling out the true hypothesis simply on the basis of a philosophical presupposition [a personal bias] for which we have no justification."

As we will see later regarding the resurrection of Christ, Dr. Gary Habermas argues that "a naturalistic theory has to, by definition, fill in the blank. A naturalistic theory is not, 'You Christians are crazy! Things like this don't happen. I don't see miracles in my life and Jesus wasn't raised from the dead.' That's not a naturalistic theory. That's a denial.

"A true naturalistic theory says, 'No, I'll tell you. Jesus didn't rise from the dead. What really happened is…fill in the blank.' A skeptic has a naturalistic theory when he or she fills in that blank. He or she is going to take these facts and give an alternative explanation."

| Some Well-Known Miracles of Jesus[6] | |
|---|---|
| **MIRACLE** | **SCRIPTURE PASSAGE** |
| Turns water into wine | John 2:1-11 |
| Orders the wind and waves to be quiet | Mark 4:35-41 |
| Walks on water | Matthew 14:22-33 |
| With five loaves and two fishes, feeds a crowd of about 5,000 people | Matthew 14:13-21 |
| Raises Lazarus to life | John 11:17-44 |
| Raises a dead girl to life | Matthew 9:18-26 |
| Gives sight to a man born blind | John 9:1-41 |
| Cures the woman who had been bleeding for 12 years | Matthew 9:20-22 |

| | |
|---|---|
| Cures a man of evil spirits | Mark 5:1-20 |
| Heals ten men with leprosy | Luke 17:11-19 |
| Heals a crippled man | Mark 2:1-12 |
| Heals a man who was deaf and could hardly talk | Mark 7:31-37 |
| Heals the high priest's servant after the man's ear is cut off | Luke 22:49-52 |

## Indicators Outside the New Testament

Consider this about miracles: Facts from psychiatry, medicine, and science supply evidence that may indicate miracles are happening in our world today. I interviewed three researchers about these new findings and was surprised at the abundance of current information that is beginning to show support for the possibility that miracles occur.

### *Indicators from Psychiatry and Medicine*

For example, Dr. Habermas said, "Another factor in favor of the miracles in the New Testament is that there is some very hard data that is difficult to explain away. I think of Marcus Borg, who reports in one of his books on Jesus that there was a team of psychiatrists recently who could not explain a couple of possession cases by normal scientific means. I also refer to a double-blind experiment with almost 400 heart patients in San Francisco who were monitored in 26 categories, and those who were prayed for were statistically better in 21 out of 26 categories. Because the experiment was performed well, the results were published in a secular journal, *The Southern Journal of Medicine.*

"So, if you can see some of these things today, maybe you can't say, 'Oh, there's a miracle right there,' but it makes you wonder a little bit. I have to say, can we thus be so quick to condemn the things Jesus did in the first century?"

*Indicators from Science*

Science is also finding evidence that points to the existence of God. If we admit to the possibility God exists, then we must be open to the possibility that miracles can happen.

Dr. William Lane Craig pointed out, "It's interesting to note that in modern science, for example, in physics, scientists are quite willing to talk about realities that are quite literally metaphysical in nature—realities that are beyond our space and time dimensions; realities that we cannot directly perceive or know but that we may infer by certain signposts of transcendence in the universe to something beyond them.

"A growing number of scientists now believe that the evidence for the big bang theory points to a simultaneous beginning for all matter, energy, and even the space-time dimensions of the universe. This evidence has led them to place the cause of the universe independent of matter, energy, space, and time. This evidence calls for the strong possibility of the existence of God."

According to William Lane Craig, "If there is a Creator and Designer of the universe, who has brought it into being, then clearly he could intervene in the course of history and perform miraculous acts. So in the absence of some sort of a proof of atheism, *it seems to me that we have to be open to the possibility of miracles.*

"To give an analogy, in the field of cosmology, the evidence indicates that the universe came into existence in a great explosion called the big bang at some point in the finite past. Many physicists are quite willing to say that this event required the existence of a transcendent Creator and Designer of the universe who brought it into being. Now, when we come to the life and ministry of Jesus of Nazareth, could it be that this same being has intervened in history in a dramatic and miraculous way as Jesus claimed? Shouldn't we at least be open to investigating those claims?"

## What Does It All Mean?

In light of the multiple attestations of historical evidence in the

Gospels that Jesus performed miracles, and in light of the evidence from non-Christian sources that Jesus was a miracle worker, and because psychiatry, medicine, and science are now reporting data that are signposts of something beyond what we know, is anyone justified in ruling out that the miraculous can occur *before* investigating the evidence?

A better approach, according to William Lane Craig, is this: "Perhaps these miracles in the life of Jesus are signposts of transcendence to something beyond the known universe....It seems to me that as open-minded people, we simply cannot exclude this in advance without looking at the evidence." As the famous physicist Sir George Stokes said, "It may be that the event which we call a miracle was brought on not by a suspension of the laws in ordinary operation, but by the super addition of something not ordinarily in operation."[7]

So if we can agree that Jesus performed miracles, then the next logical question is this: What do these miracles say about who he is? More importantly, what did Jesus think about himself? Did he really claim to be God? Keep reading...as we discover what Jesus claimed about himself.

# Did He Really Believe He Was God's Son?

**6**

*"Wasn't Jesus just a good spiritual teacher?"*

**M**any suggest Jesus was a great guy, a man of high morals. They say that his example is worth following. Certainly someone who would help the poor, heal the sick, and give his life in sacrifice for those whom he loved provides a strong symbolic reference for those seeking spiritual role models. But what if Jesus is more than all that?

Would a good spiritual teacher claim that he is *the* way, *the* truth, and *the* life, as John records?[1] Would a role model tell people that the future destiny of the world was in his hands?[2] Could a man of high morals teach that a person's belief in him determined that person's eternity in heaven or hell? People who make these kinds of claims are typically labeled as religious fanatics, radicals, or even worse.

I (John) presented these questions to a panel of scholars during a television broadcast called "Did Jesus Ever Claim to Be God?" Before we wrestle with the actual words of Jesus from the four Gospels and the responses of his audience, let's take a moment to consider what today's experts suggest regarding Christ's claims about himself.

## Considering the Issue

After Jesus began his ministry, he traveled to the city of Capernaum along the Sea of Galilee. Archaeologists tell us that Simon Peter also lived there with his family. They have found the remains of Peter's house and determined that one of the rooms was used as a house church. I (John) traveled to Capernaum and viewed the ruins of a Jewish synagogue where Jesus opened and read the scriptures about himself and performed an exorcism. This synagogue overlooks Peter's house, possibly the place where Jesus said and did something that Matthew, Mark, and Luke all record.

### "Your Sins Are Forgiven"

One of the most startling statements Jesus made was at Capernaum, when he said to a paralyzed man, "Take heart, son; your sins are forgiven."[3] The Jewish leaders claimed the statement was blasphemy. According to Jewish theology, even the Messiah couldn't forgive sins. In their worldview, only *God* could. Jesus provocatively used this statement to address the very question of who he claimed to be. It was a direct reference to his claim as deity.

Dr. Claire Pfann, a professor in Israel, observed that "the right to forgive sins is a right that belongs only to God. Jesus, in his healing power, whether he heals or whether he forgives sins, is still executing a divine imperative, a divine privilege." Whether through healing or forgiveness, Jesus displayed attributes that belong to God alone.

### Multiple Early Sources

Later in our "Did Jesus Ever Claim to Be God?" broadcast, I (John) asked Dr. N.T. Wright, "Did Jesus ever come right out and claim to have a relationship with God that no one else possessed—a relationship that legitimately gave Jesus the right to call himself the Son of God?" Wright responded, "Jesus does talk about himself as the Son of God: 'Whoever acknowledges me before men, I will also acknowledge him before *my Father* in heaven.'[4] And there is also Jesus' statement about not knowing when the destruction of

Jerusalem will take place, but 'only *the Father*'⁵ knows. So Jesus talks about himself as the Son of God in ways that it doesn't look as though the early church would ever have made up."

Dr. Gary Habermas, in another interview, explained how multiple sources documenting these claims affirm the fact Jesus claimed to be the Son of God. "In Matthew 11:27 and its parallel in Luke we have a passage that comes from what the critics call *Q,* an early sayings document. They believe this predates the Gospels by decades. Yet in Matthew 11:27 and its parallel Jesus says, 'No one knows the Son except the Father, and no one knows the Father except the Son and those to whom the Son chooses to reveal him.' Jesus is claiming unique knowledge of God, and this is found in the very early Q strata, according to the way the critics arrange this.

"The reason Matthew 24:36 is a strong verse affirming that Jesus is the Son of God is that he says he *himself* doesn't know the time of his coming back to earth. My point is this: If the church is making this statement up and putting these words into the mouth of Jesus, why do they have him saying something that is theologically embarrassing? Why would they let the Son of God say, 'I don't know the time of my coming'?

"Because if Jesus really is the Son of God, why doesn't he know the time of his coming? That can be explained by the fact Jesus had a human nature and a divine nature. But regardless, Matthew 24:36 does not seem like it can be made up because it's too embarrassing. That's a rough statement. Which makes it more likely Jesus probably said it."⁶

## The Significance of "Abba"

Jesus also referred to God the Father as "Abba" in Mark 14:36—a term of endearment used by a child to his or her father. Is this also evidence that Jesus thought he had a special relationship with God?

According to Dr. Ben Witherington, professor of New Testament at Asbury Seminary, "*Abba* means 'father.' It's not quite like 'daddy,' but it means 'father dearest.' It implies an intimate relationship with one's heavenly parent. Jesus believed he had that unique kind of relationship, which made him in some unique and special sense the Son of God.

"There's plenty of evidence for this relationship. It's in the synoptic Gospels, the Gospel of John, and the Pauline letters. It's all over the New Testament. It's one of the most characteristic things predicated of Jesus—that he was the Son of God."

### *"But I Tell You..."*

Further indication of who Jesus claimed to be is found in the Sermon on the Mount.[7] On a hillside near the Sea of Galilee is a place where Jesus preached this famous sermon. During this message, Jesus says, "You have heard that it was said, 'Do not commit adultery.' But I tell you that anyone who looks at a woman lustfully has already committed adultery with her in his heart."[8] In saying this, Jesus didn't quote some other authority in the way that the Jewish religious leaders and scribes did; rather, he spoke of himself as the authority. At the end of the sermon, we read that "when Jesus had finished saying these things, the crowds were amazed at his teachings, for he was teaching them as one having authority and not as their scribes."[9] What kind of authority did Jesus have?

Dr. Darrell Bock summarized this authority when he commented, "He forgave sin. He told the Jews what they could and could not do on the Sabbath. The Sabbath is one of the Ten Commandments. You don't mess with the Ten Commandments unless you have authority.

"He talked about who we should and should not be associated with. He claimed that he could sit at the right hand of the Father. There's not any person who gets to go directly into God's presence and park there. You must have a lot of authority and a lot of nerve to think that you can sit next to God."

### Jesus' Words

If someone claimed to be God, or God's son, the friends of that person would likely indicate those claims in their writings. We find that of the four Gospel writers, the apostle John provides perhaps the most direct teachings on this subject. Here we'll take a look at four clear case studies from John and Mark's Gospels regarding the claims of Jesus.

*Case Study #1: Mark 14*

Matthew, Mark, and Luke all record that while Jesus was on trial during the night before his crucifixion, he testified that he was God. How did he do it? In this case, these four titles were used in relation to or by Jesus:

> Again the high priest asked him, "Are you the *Christ* [Messiah], *the Son of the Blessed One* [Son of God]?"
>
> "*I am* [Exodus 3:14]," said Jesus. "And you will see *the Son of Man* sitting at the right hand of the Mighty One and coming on the clouds of heaven."[10]

Mark wrote that Jesus claimed to the Jewish Sanhedrin during his trial that he was the Christ (the Greek word for Messiah), the Son of the Blessed One (meaning "Son of God"), the "I am" (a title for God's name), and calls himself the Son of Man. Why is this significant?

The phrase "Son of Man" was unused in Jewish culture *before* Jesus' day. It was also not commonly used by Jews or Christians *after* Jesus' earthly life. There was no reason for someone who lived after Jesus to write this back into his life story. Jesus used this phrase of himself 81 times in the Gospels, and it is never used by anyone *but* Jesus. Outside of the Gospels, it is used only twice, both in reference to Jesus himself.[11]

However, the prophet Daniel used this phrase over 500 years before Jesus lived on earth. When Jesus was on trial, the Jewish Sanhedrin understood that he was claiming to be the one Daniel spoke about in these words from the book of Daniel:

> In my vision at night I looked, and there before me was one like *a son of man,* coming with the clouds of heaven. He approached the Ancient of Days and was led into his

presence. He was given authority, glory and sovereign power; all peoples, nations and men of every language worshiped him. His dominion is an everlasting dominion that will not pass away, and his kingdom is one that will never be destroyed.[12]

*Case Study #2: John 8*

In an earlier incident, we see Jesus with a different audience who had a similar reaction. During an encounter in which Jesus sent away a demon, the crowd shouted:

> "Now we know you are possessed by a demon. Even Abraham and the prophets died, but you say, 'Anyone who obeys my teaching will never die!' Are you greater than our father Abraham? He died, and so did the prophets. *Who do you think you are?*"[13]

Jesus responded with these provocative words: "Your father Abraham rejoiced as he looked forward to my coming. He saw it and was glad."[14]

Suddenly this Jewish audience couldn't believe what they were hearing. Jesus was not even 50 years old, yet he claimed to have seen Abraham? What's wrong with this guy?

Jesus then closed by saying, "I tell you the truth, before Abraham was even born, *I am!*"[15] The angry mob became incensed as they understood Jesus' clear reference to himself as God from the narrative of Moses and the burning bush.

In that story, which takes place at a burning bush in Exodus 3, Moses was told that the name of God he should use was "I am." Here in John 8, Jesus claims the same name, clearly attempting to connect himself with the "I am" from Exodus 3.

The crowd's response communicated their understanding that Jesus had claimed to be God. He must be brought to justice for such blasphemy! In condemnation, "At that point they picked up stones to throw at him."[16] Jesus slipped away, but his words were not forgotten. Now he was a marked man.

*Case Study #3: John 10*

One of the most specific Bible passages on the issue of Jesus' identity can be found in chapter 10 of John's Gospel. As Jesus walked through the Jewish temple, some Jewish leaders demanded of him, "If you are the Messiah, tell us plainly."[17]

Jesus' response was remarkably clear:

> I have already told you, and you don't believe me. The proof is the work I do in my Father's name. But you don't believe me because you are not my sheep. My sheep listen to my voice; I know them, and they follow me. *I give them eternal life,* and they will never perish. No one can snatch them away from me, for my Father has given them to me, and he is more powerful than anyone else. No one can snatch them from the Father's hand. *The Father and I are one.*[18]

According to the law of Moses, anyone who declared himself to be God was worthy of execution. And the Jews listening to Jesus clearly had a problem. They understood that Jesus was calling God *my* Father rather than *our* Father. He was teaching that he could give eternal life to people. The result?

> Once again *the people picked up stones to kill him.* Jesus said, "At my Father's direction I have done many good works. For which one are you going to stone me?" They replied, "We're stoning you not for any good work, but for blasphemy! *You, a mere man, claim to be God.*"[19]

Bottom line? Jesus claimed to be God. And his audience wanted to punish him for it.

In an interview I (John) conducted on Jesus' claim as Messiah, I asked Dr. Claire Pfann of the University of the Holy Land for her response to scholars who suggest Jesus' disciples created the idea of a divine Jesus.

Dr. Pfann said, "I think that is laughable in the face of Jewish literature from the second temple period. We have to look at the

Dead Sea Scrolls, for example, to see the messianic hope that existed among Jews before the coming of Jesus. We recognize, of course, things like Cave 4, Qumran, Manuscript 521—in which it says that when the Messiah comes, he will heal the blind, he will heal the lame, and he will raise the dead.

"We see the same claim given by Jesus himself in Luke chapter 7 when John the Baptist sends his disciples to ask Jesus, 'Are you it? The real thing? Or do we wait for somebody else?' Jesus says, 'Tell John what you've seen: the blind are healed, the lame walk, and the dead are raised.' This is a pre-Christian, Jewish messianic expectation that finds its fulfillment in Jesus."[20]

Another scholar in this same program, Dr. Craig Evans, shared a similar response to his evaluation of the Jesus Seminar materials: "I think a good example of where the Jesus Seminar is inconsistent in their own criteria is the whole question of Jesus' messianic self-understanding. They assume that this is the early church reading back into the Gospels. Here's the problem with this. You have multiple attestation. Everywhere in the tradition, Jesus is regarded as the Messiah—in all four Gospels, in the epistles, everything in the New Testament. How in the world could that emerge in the aftermath of Easter if Jesus had never claimed to be Messiah and had never allowed his following to think of that? Where does all of this come from?

"Another criterion is the criterion of result. How do you explain that? Or, another way of putting it is, 'Where there's smoke, there's usually fire.' Everybody is calling him the Messiah after Easter. Where did that come from? Probably from the 'fire' of Jesus himself in his ministry before Easter."[21]

*Case Study #4: John 14*

Here we see Jesus sharing a meal with his closest followers, the disciples. During their time together, Jesus predicted that Peter, one of his leading followers, would soon deny him. Then turning to Thomas, Jesus comforted him with the statement that he was, "the way, the truth, and the life."[22] Many people don't realize that

Jesus claimed to be the only way to God. He made that clear in this verse.

In the mix, Philip asked Jesus to show them the Father. Jesus then gave this bold response:

> Have I been with you all this time, Philip, and yet you still don't know who I am? *Anyone who has seen me has seen the Father!* So why are you asking me to show him to you? Don't you believe that I am in the Father and the Father is in me? The words I speak are not my own, but my Father who lives in me does his work through me.[23]

Philip was an orthodox Jew. As such, he believed there was only one God. Yet here, for a fourth time, Jesus clearly indicated *he* is God. In this case, instead of responding with stones, his followers grappled with the mind-blowing significance of Jesus' words. Soon afterwards, Jesus led them to the Mount of Olives, where he was arrested. His followers fled for safety, abandoning him just as predicted. They didn't have to condemn him this time. Others had already made the arrangements.

These case studies make it extremely clear that according to the Gospel writers, Jesus believed and clearly communicated to others that he was God's Son and was God himself.

## The Responses of Jesus' Audience

The Jewish leaders mentioned in John 8 and 10 weren't the only ones who understood that Jesus claimed to be God. Many others, ranging from the poorest beggars to the most affluent civic authorities, picked up on the concept that Jesus was not just a spiritual leader but spoke as if he was *the* spiritual leader of the world![24]

### Jesus in the Temple

In Matthew 21, Jesus displayed his anger at those who had commercialized Jewish worship at the temple. As he flipped over tables and released wild animals, he shouted, "The Scriptures declare, 'My Temple will be called a house of prayer,' but you have turned it into a den of thieves!"[25]

| WAS JESUS HUMAN OR DIVINE? YES, HE WAS.[26] | |
|---|---|
| **GOD** | **MAN** |
| Jesus is worshiped (Matthew 2:2,11; 14:33; 28:9) | Jesus worshiped the Father (John 17) |
| Jesus is prayed to (Acts 7:59; 1 Corinthians 1:1-2) | Jesus prayed to the Father (John 17:1) |
| Jesus was called God (John 20:28; Hebrews 1:8) | Jesus was called man (Mark 15:39; John 19:5) |
| Jesus was called Son of God (Mark 1:1) | Jesus was called Son of Man (John 9:35-37) |
| Jesus is sinless (Hebrew 4:15; 1 Peter 2:22) | Jesus was tempted (Matthew 4:1) |
| Jesus knew all things (John 21:17) | Jesus grew in wisdom (Luke 2:52) |
| Jesus gives eternal life (John 20:28) | Jesus died (Romans 5:8) |
| The fullness of deity dwells in Jesus (Colossians 2:9) | Jesus had a body of flesh and bones (Luke 24:39) |

Afterwards, the crowd praised Jesus, including numerous children. This again sparked controversy among the religious leaders. Didn't Jesus even know the first of the Ten Commandments? He could not accept their worship. He was just a man, not God.

They confronted Jesus, asking, "Do you hear what these children are saying?"

Jesus replied, "Haven't you ever read the Scriptures? For they say, 'You have taught children and infants to give you praise.'"[27] Here he referred to Psalm 8, a hymn of praise *to God*. By acknowledging the children's worship, he affirmed their belief in him as deity. While this exchange is perhaps too subtle for our culture to understand, this was a spiritual slap in the face of the Jewish religious leaders, who became more motivated than ever in their pursuit of punishment for Jesus.

### Jesus with His Friends

Matthew 16 records the earliest point at which Jesus revealed his claim to be the Jewish Messiah. In a crude first-century opinion poll, Jesus asked his followers, "Who do people say that the Son of Man is?"[28]

A sampling of responses was provided. Elijah? John the Baptist? Jeremiah? One of the prophets? Each person had formed his or her own opinion based on the recent works of this mysterious miracle man from Nazareth.

"But who do *you* say I am?"[29] Jesus gets personal at this point with his friends. The question is no longer put to other people, but to his own people, his 12 disciples.

Peter, in brash boldness, speaks up: "You are the Messiah, the Son of the living God."[30] As one writer has stated, "Here was a perfect opportunity for Jesus to dispel this growing idea that he was something other than just a great man. But Jesus wouldn't do that. Instead, he commended Peter for his declaration."[31]

Rather than *contradict* Peter, Jesus *confirmed* his words: "You are blessed, Simon son of John, because my Father in heaven has revealed this to you."[32] Why was Peter blessed? Because Jesus agreed with Peter that he was God's very son, the Messiah, the living God.

### Jesus with Thomas

Another conversation between Jesus and one of his closest friends makes it clearer that Jesus considered himself worthy of divine worship. In John 20 we find ten of Jesus' closest followers telling people that Jesus has risen from the dead three days after his crucifixion. But Thomas was a skeptic. He demanded more than the words of his beleaguered buddies to convince him that a bloodied dead body was now walking around Jerusalem. In his words, "I won't believe it unless I see the nail wounds in his hands, put my fingers into them, and place my hand into the wound in his side."[33]

Eight days later Thomas and his friends are hanging out in a locked room, still precautious against the same enemies who had earlier attempted to kill Jesus for claiming to be God. John tells the story:

> Suddenly, as before, Jesus was standing among them. "Peace be with you," he said. Then he said to Thomas, "Put your finger here, and look at my hands. Put your hand into the wound in my side. *Don't be faithless any longer. Believe!*"
>
> "My Lord and my God!" Thomas exclaimed.[34]

As Jesus showed Thomas his hands and side, the evidence caused Thomas's skepticism to melt into belief in Jesus as God.

Jesus then offered an amazing statement on the issue of faith: "You believe because you have seen me. Blessed are those who believe without seeing me."[35] This means that those who believe today base *their* faith on the testimony of those who heard and saw the risen Jesus.

---

I am trying here to prevent anyone saying the really foolish thing that people often say about Him: "I'm ready to accept Jesus as a great moral teacher, but I don't accept his claim to be God." That is the one thing we must not say. A man who was merely a man and said the sort of things Jesus said would not be a great moral teacher. He would either be a lunatic—on a level with the man who says he is a poached egg—or else he would be the Devil of Hell. You must make your choice. Either this man was, and is, the Son of God; or else a madman or something worse. You can shut Him up for a fool, you can spit at Him and kill Him as a demon, or you can fall at His feet and call Him Lord and God.

—**C.S. LEWIS,** *MERE CHRISTIANITY*[36]

---

Jesus, at the beginning of his public ministry, responded to an enticement from Satan with these words from Moses: "You must *worship the Lord your God and serve only him.*"[37] A closer look at Matthew's Gospel reveals a carefully placed note about the end of Jesus' earthly life: "Then the eleven disciples left for Galilee, going to the mountain where Jesus had told them to go. When they saw him, *they worshiped him.*"[38]

The followers of Jesus clearly believed he was God. They worshiped him. They invested the remainder of their lives communicating the message of Jesus. Yet even at the close of Matthew's Gospel, we are told that "some doubted!"[39] When they saw the risen Jesus, alive from the dead, the overwhelming significance of this was hard for them to embrace. Maybe that describes you right now. Perhaps the evidence is beginning to make sense, but to accept that Jesus is God is an overwhelming thought. But what if he *is* God?

In our next chapter, we'll take a look at the personality of Jesus. Was his life marked by any inconsistencies, any psychological problems, any signs of self-delusions? The answers to these questions hold the utmost value in helping us decide whether Jesus really is the big deal his friends claimed he was. They are also valuable for those of us who are trying to determine whether to follow Jesus.

# Was He Just Making Up This Stuff?

**7**

An intriguing editorial showed up one morning in the hands of thousands of readers of *The Oregonian* newspaper. It read:

> He promised his own resurrection ("Hereafter shall the Son of Man sit on the right hand of the power of God") and had the effrontery to forgive sins that people committed against God or others ("Son, be of good cheer; thy sins be forgiven thee"). Beyond all this, Jesus was very clear, judgmental even, about what he believed was necessary to upgrade a human being: "I am the light of the world: he that followeth me shall not walk in darkness, but shall have the light of life."
>
> Now, you don't need to believe any of this. You're free to conclude it's all total rubbish. But it's impossible to maintain Jesus is just "Mr. Nice Guy" and one of history's great moral teachers. "The Domesticated Jesus" doesn't hold up logically. He's either lord or lunatic. He can't be both.
>
> I suppose you could say you believe certain things he's said to have said and disbelieve others. But this seems arbitrary and makes about as much sense as saying you believe some wack job also happens to be one of the world's great moral teachers.[1]

Apparently the above writer says the only options that really make sense are to believe that Jesus is either God or a lunatic. While this forces out other opinions (Was he a liar? Misrepresented by his followers?), it is clear that the issue of whether Jesus was mentally challenged must be discussed in any serious conversation about who Jesus really was and is.

Could Jesus have just *thought* he was God? After all, it is possible to be both sincere and *wrong*.

---

### According to Experts...

"It is not His teachings which make Jesus so remarkable, although these would be enough to give Him distinction. It is a combination of the teachings with the man Himself. The two cannot be separated."

—**KENNETH SCOTT LATOURETTE**, FORMER HISTORIAN OF CHRISTIANITY AT YALE UNIVERSITY[2]

---

Usually such discussions begin with ten ways Jesus could not have been insane or pile up a mound of quotes from various scholars and experts to "prove" his sanity and ultimately, his deity. But what if we actually discussed the possibility? What would Jesus have been required to do for us to conclude he was deluded? Let's take a walk through five key questions that can help us better assess the personality of Jesus.

## How Did Jesus' Family and Friends Understand His Personality?[3]

Jesus' family reacted strongly when he first began to draw public attention through his miracles, healings, and teaching. Mark mentioned that "Jesus entered a house, and again a crowd gathered, so that he and his disciples were not even able to eat. When his family heard about this, they went to take charge of him, for they said, 'He is out of his mind.'"[4]

This situation would soon change. Jesus' mother, Mary, would later stand by Jesus at the cross and serve as a founding member of the church at Pentecost. His skeptical brothers James and Jude had not believed in him during his earthly life. Yet they later declared their allegiance to Jesus as the Messiah and wrote letters included in the New Testament. James would even give his life for his beliefs and his leadership in the Jerusalem church. But what caused such a change of attitude?

## Was Jesus Out of His Mind?

"When you study the life of Jesus, He clearly does not display the characteristics of insanity. The abnormality and imbalance we find in a deranged person are not there. His teachings, such as the Sermon on the Mount, remain one of the greatest works ever recorded. Jesus was continually challenged by the Pharisees and lawyers, highly educated men whose modern day equivalent would be our university professors. They were fluent in several languages and were known for their scholarship of the Old Testament and Jewish law. They challenged Jesus with some of the most profound questions of their day and Jesus' quick answers amazed and silenced them. In the face of tremendous pressure, we find He exemplified the greatest composure."

—PAT ZUKERAN[5]

At least three things transformed Jesus' family's attitudes regarding his mental state. First, they *experienced his miracles and healings*. It's hard to argue against changed lives. Those who stood alongside a man born blind who could now see found it difficult to suggest the healer was a lunatic.

Jesus' family also *encountered his unparalleled teachings*. When the crowds heard him speak, their response was that, "The crowds were amazed at his teaching, because he taught as one who had authority, and not as their teachers of the law."[6] Apparently at some later time, Jesus' family no longer saw him as being out of his mind. Rather, they saw him as being of sound mind.

Third, Jesus' family *embraced the resurrection*. When the apostle Paul wrote on the issue of the resurrection, he noted this significant point:

> He appeared to Peter, and then to the Twelve. After that,
> he appeared to more than five hundred of the brothers at

the same time, most of whom are still living, though some have fallen asleep. *Then he appeared to James,* then to all the apostles, and last of all he appeared to me also, as to one abnormally born.[7]

We can gain additional insights from the four biographies written by Jesus' friends. The lunatic lacks the very qualities that Jesus embodied—spiritual wisdom, masterful storytelling and teaching skills, tough love, and deep compassion. Almost anyone who studies the life of Jesus acknowledges that he was wise and that he was good. But if he was truly misguided in his thinking, we wouldn't have seen the sharp thinking skills and wholesome values communicated through the ancient sources of Jesus' friends.

### Could a Misguided Jew Teach Like This?

"When the crowds heard this, they were astonished at his teaching" (Matthew 22:33).

"The people were amazed at his teaching" (Mark 1:22).

"What is this? A new teaching—and with authority!" (Mark 1:27).

"The whole crowd was amazed at his teaching" (Mark 11:18).

"They were amazed at his teaching, because his message had authority" (Luke 4:32).

"All the people were amazed and said to each other, 'What is this teaching? With authority and power he gives orders to evil spirits and they come out!'" (Luke 4:36).

"They insisted, 'He stirs up the people all over Judea by his teaching. He started in Galilee and has come all the way here'" (Luke 23:5).

## How Did Jesus' Enemies Feel Around Him?

In the same passage where Mark mentions that Jesus' family thought he was out of his mind, we read that the religious leaders circulated the rumor that Jesus' miracles were accomplished by the power of Satan. They did not deny his miracle working, just the source of his power. They accused Jesus of being possessed by demons: "And the teachers of the law who came down from Jerusalem said, 'He is possessed by Beelzebub! By the prince of demons he is driving out demons.'"[8] Jesus responded by asking, "Why would Satan send away his own forces?" His accusation was that the religious leaders contradicted themselves through circular reasoning.

One writer puts it this way:

> When we meet a lunatic, we are uncomfortable because we feel vastly superior to him; when his enemies met Jesus, they were uncomfortable for the opposite reason. A lunatic does not make you feel personally challenged, only embarrassed and, eventually, bored.[9]

If Jesus was really out of his mind, then how could he debate the top scholars of his day and silence their arguments? How could he attract thousands of people to his spiritual teachings? According to the accounts we have of Jesus' enemies, they feared his thinking and teachings because they threatened their lifestyle, not because they were concerned for Jesus' mental health.

## Would Jews Really Believe a Madman Who Claimed to Be God?

If Jesus had been deluded about his claim to be God, how would people have likely responded to him? Would they violently execute a person based on his mental health? Not likely. Jewish culture traditionally showered high levels of compassion on those in need. Yet with Jesus, spiritual leaders displayed hostility of a highly political nature.

Monotheistic Jews clearly distinguished between the human and divine. The reason they wanted to put Jesus to death was because he claimed to be divine. After Jesus was arrested, the religious court challenged his claim to be God's son:

> They [the religious leaders] all asked, "Are you then the
> Son of God?"

He replied, "You are right in saying I am."

Then they said, "Why do we need any more testimony? *We have heard it from his own lips.*"[10]

The accusations against Jesus were based on what he taught. To suggest that a mentally unstable individual would teach at such a level as to draw national attention as part of a conspiracy is highly unlikely.

"Is such an intellect—clear as the sky, bracing as the mountain air, sharp and penetrating as a sword, thoroughly healthy and vigorous, always ready and always self-possessed—liable to a radical and most serious delusion concerning his own character and mission? Preposterous imagination!"

—PHILIP SCHAFF, CHURCH HISTORIAN[11]

## Did Jesus Suffer from a Divinity Complex?

A "divinity complex" is recognized as a form of psychopathology. Its character traits are well known: egotism, narcissism, inflexibility, dullness, predictability, inability to understand and love others as they really are, and to creatively relate to others. In other words, this is the exact *opposite* of the personality described of Jesus.

Someone with an inflated ego generally does not show compassion. Yet the biographical accounts of Jesus show him to be very compassionate:

- "When he saw the crowds, *he had compassion on them,* because they were harassed and helpless, like sheep without a shepherd."[12]

- "When Jesus landed and saw a large crowd, *he had compassion on them* and healed their sick."[13]

- "I have *compassion for these people...*"[14]

- "*Jesus had compassion on them* and touched their eyes."[15]

- "A man with leprosy came to him and begged him on his knees, 'If you are willing, you can make me clean.' *Filled with compassion,* Jesus reached out his hand and touched the man."[16]

- "When Jesus landed and saw a large crowd, *he had compassion on them.*"[17]

- "*I have compassion for these people;* they have already been with me three days and have nothing to eat."[18]

Jesus' followers made it extremely clear that he was a compassionate individual. In contrast with the scandalous and delusional religious leaders of their day (and ours!), Jesus provided a role model worthy of following.

## Did People Find Jesus Convincing and Credible?

This final question can best be answered by a look at the reactions of Jesus' audiences. We have already mentioned several stories of people impressed by his teachings. More specifically, however, we discover that a common response from those who crossed paths with Jesus was what the Greek language called *thaumazo,* a verb meaning "to wonder, to be amazed." The gospels note that...

- "*The men were amazed* and asked, 'What kind of man is this?'"[19]

- "The crowd *was amazed....*"[20]

- "The people *were amazed* when they saw the mute speaking, the crippled made well, the lame walking and the blind seeing."[21]

- "*This amazed everyone* and they praised God, saying, 'We have never seen anything like this!'"[22]

- "They were *completely amazed....*"[23]

- "They were *amazed at him.*"[24]

- "All spoke well of him and *were amazed* at the gracious words that came from his lips."[25]

- "Jesus rebuked the evil spirit, healed the boy and gave him back to his father. And *they were all amazed* at the greatness of God."[26]

- "The crowd *was amazed*."[27]

During an interview with psychologist Dr. Gary Collins, former *Chicago Tribune* journalist and bestselling author Lee Strobel asked for a clinical observation based on what history records about Jesus. Dr. Collins's words well summarize our conversation in this chapter:

> He was loving but didn't let his compassion immobilize him; he didn't have a bloated ego, even though he was often surrounded by adoring crowds; he maintained balance despite an often demanding lifestyle; he always knew what he was doing and where he was going; he cared deeply about people, including women and children, who weren't seen as being important back then; he was able to accept people while not merely winking at their sin; he responded to individuals based on where they were at and what they uniquely needed.[28]

So if we can agree that Jesus didn't come across as mentally disturbed in his efforts to claim he was God, what else should we discuss to better engage in understanding his influential impact? In our next chapter, we'll continue our conversation along a line of discussion that draws all our preceding information together as we tackle the phenomenon of prophecy as related to Jesus.

Did the events of Jesus' life merely coincide with predictions made about a Jewish Messiah hundreds of years before Jesus' time? Or is it possible that a supernatural God chose to foretell many of the specific aspects of Jesus' life to show those seeking truth that Jesus is the Messiah?

# Did His Life Really Fulfill the Predictions?

**8**

- How difficult would it be for someone to predict *the exact city* in which the birth of a future U.S. president would take place in the year A.D. 2710? That's what the prophet Micah did 700 years before Jesus was born.

- How difficult do you think it would be to indicate *the precise kind of death penalty* a new, unknown religious leader would experience of a thousand years from today? That's what David did in 1000 B.C. when he wrote Psalm 22.

- How difficult would it be to *predict the specific date* of the appearance of a specific great future leader hundreds of years in advance? That's what the prophet Daniel did 530 years before Jesus.[1]

One of the most fascinating aspects of any study of Jesus' life is that of his relationship to predictive prophecy. Through the ancient Jewish prophets, God made 456 predictions that would help people to identify Mr. X—God's special Messiah, who would come in the future.

These identifying marks separate the Messiah from everyone else to ever live on planet Earth. As we will see, every one of these specific characteristics was fulfilled in Jesus Christ.

## The One and Only

Each person on planet Earth has an address comprised of seven facts that help identify and separate that person from the other six billion people on the planet. What information separates me (John) from every person on earth? It is my home address, which contains the following information:

1. *My continent:* North America separates my *continent* from all others.

2. *My country:* The United States separates my *country* from all others.

3. *My state:* Tennessee separates my state (or province) from all others.

4. *My city:* Chattanooga separates my city from all cities in my state (or province).

5. *My zip code:* 37411 separates my zip code from all other zip codes.

6. *My street address:* This separates my address from all other addresses within my zip code.

7. *My name:* John separates me from all other family names in my home.

In the same way, specific bits of information, or prophecies, about the coming Messiah separate Jesus from all other people in history. No other person fits the details of the 456 prophecies that were given in advance of his life in the Old Testament scriptures.

David Greenglass was a World War II traitor. He gave atomic secrets to the Russians and then fled to Mexico after the war. His conspirators arranged to help him by planning a meeting with the secretary of the Russian ambassador in Mexico City. Proper identification for both parties was vital, in order to ensure that no imposters came along. Greenglass was to identify himself with six prearranged signs. These instructions had been given to both the secretary and

Greenglass so there would be no possibility of making a mistake. They were:

1. Once in Mexico City, Greenglass was to write a note to the secretary, signing his name as "I. JACKSON";

2. After three days he was to go to the Plaza de Colon in Mexico City and

3. stand before the statue of Columbus,

4. with his middle finger placed in a guide book. In addition,

5. when he was approached, he was to say it was a magnificent statue and that he was from Oklahoma.

6. The secretary was to then give him a passport.

These six prearranged signs worked. Why? With six identifying characteristics it was impossible for the secretary *not* to identify Greenglass as the proper contact.[2]

The same is true concerning Jesus Christ. The identification marks given in Bible prophecy hundreds of years in advance point to Jesus and *no one else.*

### Select Messianic Prophecies Fulfilled by Jesus

While there are hundreds of prophecies in the Jewish scriptures of the Messiah, a select few specify detailed facts that no other human could fulfill. For example, the Messiah would:

- Be male, born of a woman.[3]
- Be of Jewish heritage as a descendant from the family line of Abraham, Isaac, and Jacob.[4]
- Be from the tribe of Judah, not the other 11 tribes.[5]
- Be a prophet like Moses who must be obeyed.[6]
- Be a descendant of David.[7]
- Be the child born as God with an everlasting kingdom.[8]

- Be born in the small town of Bethlehem.[9]

- Have a messenger who would precede him and prepare the way for him.[10]

- Die a humiliating death.[11]

- Be "cut off" 483 years after the decree given to Nehemiah to rebuild Jerusalem.[12]

- Be crushed and pierced for our transgressions.[13]

- Die to pay for every person's sin.[14]

- Be called "the one they have pierced."[15]

- Be betrayed for 30 pieces of silver.[16]

- Be executed with criminals as an innocent man.[17]

- Have his hands and feet pierced.[18]

- Have his side pierced.[19]

- Be buried in a rich man's tomb.[20]

- Be raised from the dead.[21]

What is the possibility of someone fulfilling just these 19 prophecies by chance? The science of probability attempts to determine the chance of a predicted event's occurrence.

## Probability Theory in Practice

Imagine someone placing 100 Ping-Pong balls in a barrel and marking one of the balls with an X. Next he stirs up all the balls in the barrel, blindfolds you, and asks you to reach down and pick out that one ball with the X. What are your chances? One chance in 100.

Now, selecting a Ping-Pong ball may seem an unimportant thing. But what if we told you that there was one chance out of 100 that the airplane you were about to board would safely reach its destination? Would you still want to fly? Of course not.

If there were 1,000 balls in a much larger barrel, you would have a much smaller chance of choosing the right ball. The chance of successfully picking out the right ball would be one in 1,000.

Now imagine there are a *million* balls filling a stadium. Your chance of reaching into a million balls and picking out the right one would be extremely small. Your chance would be one in 1,000,000. Mathematically, this number would be 10 to the 6th power. But still, it would be possible. People do win the lottery (and their chances are also built on the probability theory). But could you pick out the same ball three times in a row? That would be the equivalent of three prophecies coming true in the future.

### Probability and Prophecy

But let's make the stakes a little higher. How many balls would we have to put in a stadium if the chance of picking out the right ball was one out of 10 to the 17th power? This is the number that has been calculated for the fulfillment of just eight prophecies in the life of Jesus. How big of a number is this?

Dr. Stoner gives the answer using this illustration.[22] First, cover the entire state of Texas with silver dollars to a level of two feet deep. Then get in an airplane and fly over the state of Texas. Somewhere along the way, drop one silver dollar that is marked with an X. Then thoroughly stir all the silver dollars that cover the state of Texas.

Then blindfold a man and tell him that he can walk anywhere he wishes in the state of Texas for three months. Sometime during his walking he must stop, reach down into the two feet of silver dollars he is standing upon, and pick out the one silver dollar that was marked with an X. The chance of that man finding that one silver dollar would be one out of 10 to the 17th power.

### Probability and Possibility

Remember, there are *456 specific prophecies* of the Messiah in the Old Testament.[23] To simplify the numbers involved, let's calculate the chance of just 48 of those prophecies coming true about any one person in the future. What does the science of probability reveal?

Probability shows us that the chance of 48 prophecies all coming true in any one person in the future would be one in 10 to the 157th power! That's the number 10 followed by 157 zeros.

The human mind can barely even comprehend such a large number. To get an idea of what this number means, let's consider electrons, an extremely small particle. To count the number of electrons that are in a straight one-inch line, we would have to count four electrons every second *and* continue counting day and night for *19 million years*. That number would not even come close to 10 to the 157th power electrons.

To understand how enormous of a number this is, we would have to build a large ball that extends from the earth to a distance of six billion light years away. How many miles long is six billion light years? The distance in miles of just *one* light year is 6.4 trillion miles. To figure out the total distance of miles this ball measures, multiply 6.4 trillion miles times six billion light years. Whatever that number turns out to be, we would then have to fill that big ball completely full with electrons.

But wait...even if we did, we *still* don't have anywhere close to the number of electrons needed to reach the number 10 to 157th power. In order to reach that number we would have to make more large balls just as large as the first one.

How many more? *Trillions,* with each one six billion light years long and filled with electrons. Then, if we were able to add up the colossal number of electrons in trillions of huge balls, that total number of electrons would only *start* to reach the number 10 to the 157th power.

Now assuming we have enough balls to contain 10 to the 157th power electrons, imagine marking just one tiny electron with an X and placing it among all those other electrons. Then imagine stirring up all those trillions of electrons and appointing one person to travel on a rocket for as long as desired in any direction for up to 100,000 light years.

Somewhere along the way, that person must stop his spaceship, segment a square foot of mass, and bring it into his spaceship. Then he must segment a one-inch specimen from that mass, examine it with an electron microscope, and find the electron marked with an X.

What is the probability of that person finding the marked electron? The chance would be one in 10 to the 157th power—which is the same chance of any one person fulfilling only 48 of the Old Testament prophecies about the Messiah. And remember, 48 comprises just over *ten percent* of the total number of Old Testament prophecies regarding the Jewish Messiah.

---

### Impossibility Thinking?

According to French mathematician Emile Borel, once we go past one chance in 10 to the 50th power, the probability of an event happening is so small it's impossible to think it will ever occur by chance.[24]

---

What does all this mean? It's rigged. These prophecies do not point toward randomness or luck, but toward an intentional purpose regarding a particular person—Jesus Christ.

### A Look under the Hood

Even with these figures regarding probabilities, some still say, "The prophecies were so general they were easy to fulfill." But the prophecies, in fact, were quite specific, and cannot be casually dismissed. Because we don't have the time or space to walk through every prediction about Jesus, we'll focus on 12 specific prophecies and compare them to their alleged fulfillment during the life of Jesus to better determine whether they really do point to Jesus Christ.

1. *The Messiah would be born in a specific city*

The social reformer and Jewish prophet Micah proclaimed, "You, Bethlehem Ephrathah, though you are small among the clans of Judah, out of you will come for me one who will be ruler over Israel, whose origins are from of old, from ancient times."[25] When was this written? In 700 B.C.

Nearly 700 years later, Matthew records that Jesus was born in Bethlehem in Judea, during the time of King Herod.[26] Even the Jewish religious leaders alive during the time of Jesus understood Micah's prediction. When the wise men came from the East in search of this Jewish king, Herod asked the Jewish teachers of the law for this king's birthplace. Their response? "In Bethlehem in Judea...for this is what the prophet has written."[27] Who was "the prophet"? You guessed it—Micah.

## 2. The Messiah would come from one of the 12 Jewish tribes

The Hebrew patriarch Jacob was the father of 12 sons, who were the founders of the 12 tribes of ancient Israel. At his death, Jacob offered words of blessing to each son. Regarding his child Judah, he promised, "The scepter will not depart from Judah, nor the ruler's staff from between his feet, until he comes to whom it belongs and the obedience of the nations is his."[28] Sound a little vague? Not to Jewish ears. They would have understood the references to "the scepter" and "the ruler's staff" as symbols of leadership. Whoever the reference concerned, it would be a person from the family line of Judah who would serve as the greatest of leaders. This prediction in the book of Genesis was written by Moses around 1410 B.C.

Both Matthew and Luke record the family genealogy of Jesus, with one genealogy listing Joseph's family and the other Mary's family. In both accounts, the family line traced their origins to Judah, the very tribe mentioned in the prophecy by Jacob.[29] Early Christian thought quickly connected this family link with the promise made generations earlier by one of Judaism's patriarchs.

## 3. The Messiah would be preceded by a messenger

Isaiah wrote over 600 years before the birth of Jesus. In fact, one of the best finds among the Dead Sea Scrolls includes the Isaiah Scroll, which dated to approximately 200 years before the birth of Jesus.

Regarding John the Baptist, Jesus' cousin, Isaiah predicted, "A voice of one calling: 'In the desert prepare the way for the LORD; make straight in the wilderness a highway for our God.'"[30] Notice that Isaiah says this person will come *from the desert,* his message will prepare the way for the Messiah, and he even calls the coming one "God."

In Matthew's biography of Jesus, we read, "In those days John the Baptist came, preaching in the Desert of Judea, and saying, 'Repent, for the kingdom of heaven is near.'"[31] In this same chapter, Matthew shares that Jesus is the one John was speaking of, even baptizing Jesus as the Messiah began his public service. Just as Isaiah predicted, John the Baptist preached in the desert, spoke about the soon-coming Messiah, and considered Jesus as God.

4. *The Messiah would enter Jerusalem on a colt*

Luke's biography of Jesus recalls Jesus' entry into Jerusalem the week before his death. His mode of transportation? According to the historical records, Jesus rode a colt, a young donkey. What's so significant about that?

Once again, we find that someone predicted a specific event that Jesus would do. Jesus' mode of transportation was foreseen centuries earlier. The Jewish prophet Zechariah wrote, "Rejoice greatly, O Daughter of Zion! Shout, Daughter of Jerusalem! See, your king comes to you, righteous and having salvation, gentle and riding on a donkey, on a colt, the foal of a donkey."[32] While utilizing donkeys for travel was common in the first century, to have a specific reference to a "colt, the foal of a donkey" is to speak with such precision that there seems to be no other explanation than predictive prophecy. Remember, Zechariah penned these words around 550 years before the earthly life of Jesus!

5. *The Messiah would be betrayed by a friend*

Jesus was betrayed by one of his own followers, Judas, on the eve of his crucifixion. While the Gospels communicate that Jesus himself had foreknowledge of who would hand him over for death, a much earlier account also speaks about this event.

King David, in a song written a 1,000 years earlier, shares, "Even my close friend, whom I trusted, he who shared my bread, has lifted up his heel against me."[33] Who is this close friend? David probably never knew. Yet in the Gospels we read that Judas was one of Jesus' 12 closest friends, shared bread with him (including the Last Supper), and conspired against him. As Matthew remembers:

> While he was still speaking, Judas, one of the Twelve, arrived. With him was a large crowd armed with swords and clubs, sent from the chief priests and the elders of the people. Now the betrayer had arranged a signal with them: "The one I kiss is the man; arrest him." Going at once to Jesus, Judas said, "Greetings, Rabbi!" and kissed him. Jesus replied, "Friend, do what you came for." Then the men stepped forward, seized Jesus and arrested him.[34]

Could David's lyrics be only a coincidence? Perhaps one could get away with such thinking if this were the only spot to connect the Jewish scriptures with the life of Jesus. However, this is the fifth *very specific* prophetic connection we have mentioned to Jesus' life.

6. *The Messiah would be sold for 30 pieces of silver*

Matthew also shares the financial motivation behind Judas' betrayal:

> Then one of the Twelve—the one called Judas Iscariot— went to the chief priests and asked, "What are you willing to give me if I hand him over to you?" So they counted out for him thirty silver coins.[35]

Interestingly, even the specific monetary amount that would be paid was recorded in the Jewish scriptures. Zechariah acted out a calling from his God. He was commanded to "pasture the flock marked for slaughter."[36] After a dispute about his work, Zechariah ended his shepherding. In his wrap-up with his employer, he remarked, "I told them, 'If you think it best, give me my pay; but if not, keep it.' So they paid me *thirty pieces of silver.*"[37] Interestingly, this was also the price for the redemption of a servant, according to the law of Moses.[38] This visual form of teaching served as an additional prophecy of the set price for Jesus' betrayal.

### 7. *The Messiah would be spit upon and beaten*

The "servant" mentioned in Isaiah's prophecies[39]—who is understood to be the Messiah—undertakes a graphic beating in one of those prophecies: "I offered my back to those who beat me, my cheeks to those who pulled out my beard; I did not hide my face from mocking and spitting."[40] Sound familiar? Maybe because this is *exactly* the type of violent treatment Jesus received prior to his crucifixion.

Matthew details the brutality of the Jewish leaders as they accused him of blasphemy: "They *spit in his face* and *struck him* with their fists. Others slapped him and said, 'Prophesy to us, Christ. Who hit you?'"[41] Later, Roman soldiers would torture him similarly:

> They stripped him and put a scarlet robe on him, and then twisted together a crown of thorns and set it on his head. They put a staff in his right hand and knelt in front of him and *mocked him.* "Hail, king of the Jews!" they said. *They spit on him,* and took the staff and struck him on the head again and again.[42]

*Sure,* you may be thinking, *any rebel would have been treated in this way during the first century.* But notice what they called Jesus. The Jewish leaders mocked him as *the Christ.* The Roman soldiers mocked him as *King of the Jews.* This was not the treatment they would have given to an ordinary criminal. This was a religious mocking of one who claimed to be the Messiah, complete with the spitting, beating, and mocking predicted centuries earlier.

### 8. *The Messiah would be wounded by his enemies*

In a later prophecy, Isaiah also notes that the Messiah was "pierced for our transgressions, he was crushed for our iniquities;

the punishment that brought us peace was upon him, and by his wounds we are healed." [43]

Notice the specifics of this prediction. First, it included a piercing. One of my (Dillon's) favorite Christian T-shirts as a youth pastor was one that read "Body Piercing Saved My Life." While provocative, the words are true. For Christians, the pierced hands and feet of Jesus represent the suffering he endured so he could offer eternal life to them.

Second, Jesus was "crushed for our iniquities." What would it mean to be crushed? In the Gospels, we find that after the Roman governor Pilate was persuaded to execute Jesus, "he had Jesus flogged, and handed him over to be crucified." [44] A flogging would have been performed with a lead-tipped whip, and sometimes such whips were even laced with chips of bone or other sharp materials. According to Jewish tradition, 40 lashes minus one was the maximum number of lashes allowed. History also notes that criminals sometimes died during these whippings. This could definitely be classified as being "crushed."

### 9. *The Messiah would be silent before his accusers*

One striking observation made by the Gospel writers was that Jesus refused to argue for his own release before his sentencing. Pilate didn't quite know how to handle him: "'Don't you hear the testimony they are bringing against you?' But Jesus made no reply, not even to a single charge—to the great amazement of the governor." [45]

This detail was predicted long ago in the book of Isaiah: "He was oppressed and afflicted, yet he did not open his mouth; he was led like a lamb to the slaughter, and as a sheep before her shearers is silent, so he did not open his mouth." [46] Using the imagery of a lamb led to slaughter, Isaiah uniquely identifies yet another aspect of Jesus' life in stunning detail.

In fact, during one specific period of research, revisionist scholars began disputing the traditional dating of Isaiah, claiming its predictions could not have been made before the lifetime of Jesus. However, in the mid-twentieth century, the discovery of the Dead Sea Scrolls revealed an intact Hebrew Isaiah scroll from approximately 200 years before the life of Jesus. This, combined with the fact that Isaiah was translated into Greek prior to Jesus' earthly life, disproves any attempt to redate the predictions from the prophet Isaiah.

10. *The betrayal money would be thrown in the temple and given for a potter's field*

Continuing our earlier story from Zechariah, after receiving 30 coins from his employer, "The LORD said to me [Zechariah], 'Throw it to the potter'—the handsome price at which they priced me! So I took the thirty pieces of silver and threw them into the house of the LORD to the potter."[47] At first this appears to serve as a very cryptic message. What does a potter's house have to do with Jesus?

If we fast-forward to Matthew's Gospel once more, we read that Judas became overwhelmed by guilt after betraying his leader:

> When Judas, who had betrayed him, realized that Jesus had been condemned to die, he was filled with remorse. So he took the thirty pieces of silver back to the leading priests and the elders. "I have sinned," he declared, "for I have betrayed an innocent man."
>
> "What do we care?" they retorted. "That's your problem."
>
> Then Judas threw the silver coins down in the Temple and went out and hanged himself.[48]

The chief priest found themselves in a catch-22. If they invested the funds back into their treasury, they would be breaking their own law, the very law they had used to condemn Jesus. If they left the money where Judas had thrown it, someone would surely discover their involvement with Judas. Their decision? "'It is against the law to put this into the treasury, since it is blood money.' So they decided to *use the money to buy the potter's field* as a burial place for foreigners. That is why it has been called the Field of Blood to this day."[49]

Here we have yet another prediction that fits nicely. Judas was given 30 silver coins, which he threw into the temple, and the coins were used to purchase real estate from a potter. This precisely fulfills Zechariah's earlier notation of 30 coins on the floor of the Lord's house to the potter. Mere coincidence? The odds are nearly impossible.

### 11. *The Messiah would have his hands and feet pierced*

Psalm 22 finds David once again making predictions in the form of musical lyrics. Here he lamented, "Dogs have surrounded me; a band of evil men has encircled me, they have pierced my hands and my feet."[50] Those in David's day would have naturally attributed these woes to themselves, suffering Jews who were outnumbered by foes in the day of battle. Yet a more specific later account complements this verse as a prediction quite nicely.

Luke, the most detailed of Jesus' biographers, notes that during Jesus' day of death, "When they came to the place called the Skull, there they crucified him, along with the criminals—one on his right, the other on his left."[51] Notice the connections: piercing of hands and feet—just as in crucifixion; a band of evil encircled me—perhaps a reference to those hanging to the right and left of Jesus; dogs have surrounded me—possibly a reference to Jesus' enemies, since David elsewhere refers to enemies as dogs.[52]

Some have noted that the Roman method of crucifixion had not even been invented yet. For David to specifically mention the Messiah dying in this way would have been of utmost significance since it predicted a form of execution not yet in existence.

### 12. *The Messiah would be crucified with thieves*

Isaiah, speaking once more of the coming Messiah, prophesied:

> I will give him a portion among the great, and he will divide the spoils with the strong, because *he poured out his life unto death,* and was *numbered with the transgressors.* For he bore the sin of many, and made intercession for the transgressors.[53]

In Matthew we find the specific details that "two robbers were crucified with him, one on his right and one on his left."[54] Transgressors were considered lawbreakers, as were the two robbers hanging to the sides of Jesus. Interestingly, Jesus also prayed from the cross and "made intercession," as Isaiah recorded.

## Getting Personal

Louis Lapides grew up within a Jewish family in New Jersey. During a time of reflection on his own spiritual journey, he stumbled upon the realization that the Messiah of Isaiah 53 perfectly fit the portrait of Jesus of Nazareth. Now a pastor and past director of Messianic Chosen People Ministries, his studies and life experiences have led him from skepticism of Jesus to personally embracing him as Messiah in his own life.

In an interview, Lapides was asked, "If the prophecies are so obvious and point so unquestionably toward Jesus, why don't more Jews accept him as their Messiah?"

He answered, "In my case, I took the time to read them." If you haven't accepted the challenge of reading the biographies of Jesus for yourself, why not check out the rest of the story on your own? Beginning with John's Gospel, you can find out much more about Jesus and determine for yourself whether these numerous predictions are simply interesting information or something more—something you should take personally.

# Part Three

# Did Jesus Really Come Alive Again?

*"If the resurrection had not happened, then we wouldn't be here speaking. There would have been no Christian movement."*

—Dr. Edwin Yamauchi[1]

*"The evidence is there, the sources are there, the picture is clear and coherent, and, in my academic opinion, the picture is quite compelling."*

—Dr. Craig Evans[2]

The main event of Jesus' life is his resurrection from the dead. If he had not risen from the dead, it wouldn't have mattered what he taught. You can forget about Jesus and Christianity.

Why? Jesus claimed to be God, and God doesn't lie. Jesus said that he would rise from the dead on the third day. If there were no resurrection of his literal, physical body from the tomb, then he is not God and Christianity is false.

But if Jesus did rise from the dead? Then he *is* God. Christianity's message *is* true. It would indicate we should listen to him and not to someone else. In fact, the Christian faith has been willing to put itself on the line down through the centuries right at this point by saying, "If the resurrection happened, then Christianity is true. If it didn't, then Christianity is false."

A rabbinic lawyer who persecuted Christians one day encountered the risen Jesus. We know him today as the apostle Paul. He wrote to the Christians in Corinth, "If Christ has not been raised, our preaching is *useless* and so is *your faith*....If only for this life we have hope in Christ, *we are to be pitied more than all men.*"[3]

In the next five chapters, we tackle the most significant factors regarding Christ's resurrection. Included are expert insights from some of today's top scholars in the United States, Canada, the United

Kingdom, and Israel. Through their insights, we will investigate five key historical facts about the end of Jesus' life that the vast majority of critical scholars accept as true.

First, we'll discuss the death of Jesus on the cross. We will find that not only do most historians today believe it happened—they also realize the importance of verifying his death by crucifixion *before* examining his resurrection.

Next, we'll investigate the issues surrounding the honorable burial of Jesus. In the process, we'll discover why his burial is such a significant fact in confirming Jesus' literal, physical resurrection.

Third, we'll share information about the empty tomb of Jesus. This will include some of the key theories offered as to how it became empty, along with some intriguing discussions with Israeli archaeologists about first-century tombs.

Fourth, our tour will consider the historical fact that many people had multiple post-resurrection experiences involving Jesus. You may be surprised to discover how many individuals claimed to see the risen Jesus and how many times he appeared during the 40 days following his resurrection.

Finally, we'll look at the origin of the disciples' belief that Jesus rose from the dead. Something major happened that caused a rapid spread of the early church. This chapter will talk about what that something was.

Along the way, we'll hear stories from individuals whose lives were significantly altered upon understanding these aspects of Christ's life. We think you, too, will walk away with a greater appreciation of how Jesus has influenced this world...and his promises for the next.

The Death of Jesus:

# What Does the Medical Evidence Suggest?

**9**

Over the last three years, American and British television networks have aired numerous specials on the life of Jesus. Guests and scholars have issued many new opinions about what happened at the end of Jesus' life. Some of the more controversial opinions include:

- Jesus didn't really die on the cross. He survived and became a traveler to Egypt or to Europe.

- Jesus' body was secretly taken out of the tomb by his mother, Mary, and his brother, James. The disciples never discovered what they had done.

- The disciples had hallucinations of a resurrected Jesus, saw psychologically induced visions, or made up the story that Jesus came alive again to comfort others who loved Jesus and wanted to remember him in a unique way.

How can a person sift through these theories and get to the truth of what really happened at the end of Jesus' life?

I (John) discussed many of these issues during a television

program on the historical Jesus with historian and philosopher Dr. William Lane Craig.[4] A scholar of elite status, Dr. Craig has debated this topic with Dr. Bart Ehrman of Harvard University, John Dominic Crossan of the Jesus Seminar, and atheist Gerd Ludemann. Dr. Craig has also written over a dozen scholarly books on the life of Jesus Christ. Rather than arguing directly from a Christian perspective, he instead offered a consensus of historical facts agreed upon by both Christian and non-Christian scholars about the events at the end of Jesus' life.

## The Historical Foundations

I first began by asking what historical facts we must investigate to obtain a clear picture of what happened at the end of Jesus' life. In his words, "It seems to me that there are five fundamental historical facts which any credible historian must account for to give a tenable historical hypothesis about the fate of Jesus of Nazareth. The first is the death of Jesus. The second is the honorable burial of Jesus. The third is the discovery of his empty tomb. Fourth would be the postmortem appearances of Jesus. Fifth would be the origin of the disciples' belief that Jesus had risen from the dead."

*Twelve Key Facts*

Dr. Gary Habermas, whose research was shared in earlier chapters of this book, also participated in this interview. He argued that there are not only five, but rather 12 historical facts that the vast majority of today's scholars, regardless of personal bias, will typically admit about the end of Jesus' life.

According to Habermas, these 12 facts include:

1. Jesus died by crucifixion.

2. Jesus was honorably buried.

3. Jesus' death caused his followers to lose hope.

4. Jesus' tomb was soon empty.

5. Jesus' followers believed they had seen Jesus alive.

6. Jesus' followers regained hope and communicated a risen Jesus.

7. This message was the center of preaching in the early church.

8. This message was communicated in and around Jerusalem shortly after the death of Jesus.

9. The church was started and grew quickly.

10. Sunday became the primary day of worship for Christians.

11. James, a former skeptic, became an early leader of the Jerusalem church after he "believed" he had seen Jesus alive after his death.

12. Paul later had an experience with the risen Jesus and became a leader in the early Christian movement.

Having reviewed over 1,000 different scholarly sources, Habermas is able to say, "With the exception of the empty tomb, virtually all critical scholars accept these facts as historical, and most of them will even grant the empty tomb. And by the way, these facts have two prerequisites. It's not only that they are admitted by virtually all critical scholars, but they are also individually attested by other data."

*Facts About Jesus' Death*

I (John) then asked Dr. Habermas, "What do you think about those who claim Jesus didn't really die on the cross?"

He sat up in his chair and quickly responded. "Jesus *died.* Why do scholars today rarely question the death of Jesus? Why do the founders of the Jesus Seminar, for example, say that the fact that Jesus died is the surest fact we have in his career? It's because the data is so strong.

"What is some of this data? First, death by crucifixion is essentially death by asphyxiation. When you hang on a cross and the weight of your body pulls down on the intercostal pectoral and deltoid muscles around your lungs, you reach a state where, when the body's weight is dragging down on them, you can inhale, but you are increasingly unable to exhale until you reach a place of near paralysis and can't exhale at all.

"In the 1950s an experiment was performed in West Germany in which male volunteers were tied to a 2 x 4. These males lost consciousness at a maximum of 12 minutes. Now, a person nailed to a cross can push himself up on the nails to relieve the muscles in his lungs. But when he pulls down on the nails, because he can't stay up there for long, he ends up in a low position on the cross and begins to asphyxiate. The Roman centurion did not require a degree in medicine to know what was happening to the person on the cross. If the person was hanging low on the cross for any amount of time, even 30 minutes, he's dead."

What Dr. Habermas described would be enough evidence to convince most people that Jesus died on the cross. But as we researched Jesus' final 24 hours before his burial, we found that there was a lot more done to Jesus to bring him to the point of human death.

## The Medical Foundations

Based on the research conducted by several medical professionals and theological scholars, a wealth of information is currently available regarding many of the medical aspects of Jesus' death. While we will only glance at the highlights of the available reports, we will go into enough detail to confirm that Jesus was DOA—dead on arrival—at the tomb.

### The Trials

Shortly after midnight, Jesus was arrested in the garden at Gethsemane by the temple officials. Between that time and sunrise on Friday, Jesus was tried before Caiaphas and the political Sanhedrin. Here his first major physical trauma was inflicted. The guards blindfolded Jesus, spat on him, taunted him, and struck him in the face with their fists.[5] Soon after daybreak, Jesus was tried before the Sanhedrin, the body of Jewish religious leaders, who again found him guilty of blasphemy, a crime punishable by death.

Unfortunately for the Jewish leaders, only the Romans had permission to execute a traitor or conspirator. Later that morning, Jesus was taken to the Praetorium, the residence of Pontius Pilate. Pilate made no charges against Jesus and instead sent him to Herod Antipas, the tetrarch of Judea. Herod, in turn, returned Jesus to Pilate. Due to the crowd's adamant demand that Jesus be crucified, Pilate finally granted their wish. Jesus was handed over to some Roman soldiers to be whipped and then nailed to a cross.

> "His death, beyond any question of dispute, was the most famous death in human history. No other death has aroused a fraction of such intense feeling over so many hundred years. Few can be passive about Jesus. No other human being has been so loved and so hated, so adored and so despised, so proclaimed and so opposed."
>
> —DAVID WATSON, *JESUS THEN AND NOW*[6]

## The Roman Whipping

After Jesus had been turned over to Roman hands, he experienced the torture of whipping, also known as flogging or scourging. According to scholars, flogging was a legal preliminary to every Roman execution.[7] Only women and Roman senators or soldiers were exempt.[8] The usual instrument was a short whip with several single or braided leather thongs of variable lengths. Each braid contained small iron balls or sharp pieces of sheep bones tied at intervals along the leather strands.[9]

In preparation for this whipping, the individual was stripped of his clothing. The hands were tied to an upright post.[10] The back, buttocks, and legs were flogged either by two soldiers or by one soldier who alternated positions. The severity of the scourging depended on the attitude of the soldiers and was intended to weaken the victim to a state just short of collapse or death. After the scourging, the soldiers often taunted their victim.

According to one examination of the historical and medical evidence, we find the following graphic scenario:

> As the Roman soldiers repeatedly struck the victim's back with full force, the iron balls would cause deep contusions, and the leather thongs and sheep bones would cut into the skin and subcutaneous tissues. Then, as the flogging continued, the lacerations would tear into the underlying skeletal muscles and produce quivering ribbons of bleeding flesh. Pain and blood loss generally set the stage for circulatory shock. The extent of blood loss may well have determined how long the victim would survive on the cross.[11]

In the Gospel accounts, we read that Jesus was *severely* whipped. It is not known whether the number of lashes was stopped at the Jewish limit of 39. His Roman torturers may have increased the number as they saw fit. The heavy whip was brought down with full force repeatedly across Jesus' shoulders, back, and legs. At first the weighted thongs cut through the skin only. Then, as the blows continued, they cut deeper into the subcutaneous tissues, producing first an oozing of blood from the capillaries and veins of the skin and finally spurting arterial bleeding from vessels in the underlying muscles.[12]

The Roman soldiers also took particular pleasure in mocking Jesus about being a king. They placed a purple robe on him, a crown of thorns on his head, and a wooden staff in his hand. In spite, the soldiers then spat on him, punching him as well as striking him with the wooden staff. Finally they removed the robe, likely reopening his newly acquired wounds, and threw on his original garment.

According to one medical doctor's investigation of the Roman flogging, "When it was determined by the centurion in charge that the prisoner was near death, the beating was finally stopped."[13] Even before his suffering on the cross, Jesus would have already endured enough pain to soon end his human life.

Why is this important? Some people have alleged that Jesus didn't really die on the cross. He simply passed out and was later revived and able to exit the tomb, either on his own or with the help of his buddies. But the torture Jesus experienced that day would have made it physically impossible for him to have simply walked away alive. If Jesus did come out of the tomb, he came out by some other means.

## The Crucifixion

Despite the enormous cache of historical information about Jesus, some still suggest that crucifixion did not even exist during his time. In a PBS special interview, Dr. L. Michael White, professor of classics at the University of Texas, was asked, "What kind of evidence do we have for what really happened [regarding the crucifixion]?"

### A Brief History of Crucifixion

"Crucifixion probably first began among the Persians. Alexander the Great introduced the practice to Egypt and Carthage, and the Romans appear to have learned of it from the Carthaginians. Although the Romans did not invent crucifixions they perfected it as a form of torture and capital punishment that was designed to produce a slow death with maximum pain and suffering. It was one of the most disgraceful and cruel methods of execution and usually was reserved only for slaves, foreigners, revolutionaries, and the vilest of criminals. Roman law usually protected Roman citizens from crucifixion, except perhaps in the case of desertion by soldiers."

—FROM A WEB SITE ABOUT THE CRUCIFIXION[14]

His response?

Crucifixion was something very, very real. There are too many ancient sources that talk about it. Josephus himself describes a number of crucifixions that took place in Judea at about this time. So we can be fairly confident of the crucifixion as a historical event because it was a very commonplace affair in those days and very gruesome.[15]

---

### Did You Know...

...a first-century skeleton of a young man who had been crucified was discovered in ancient Palestine in 1968? He still had a large nail pierced through his feet.[16]

---

After Jesus was tortured, he, the two thieves, and some supervising Roman soldiers led by a centurion began their slow journey along the path known as the Via Dolorosa ("way of the cross"). Tied to Jesus' shoulders was the heavy crossbeam, the weight of which would have caused Jesus to stumble. And when that happened, the beam likely smacked his head and shoulders, producing additional pain. The centurion, undeterred, selected a North African man, Simon of Cyrene, to carry the cross. Jesus followed, still bleeding and sweating the cold, clammy sweat that comes from bodily shock. Traveling the length of over six football fields, Jesus journeyed from the Fortress Antonia to Golgotha. At Golgotha, Jesus was then again stripped of his clothing except for a loin cloth.

Simon placed Jesus on the soil along with the heavy beam. A soldier reached for a hammer and felt for the depression at the front of the wrist. He drove a heavy, square wrought-iron nail through Jesus' flesh and deep into the wood. Quickly he moved to the other side and repeated the action, being careful not to pull Jesus' arms too tightly, but to allow some flexion and movement. Jesus' left foot was then pressed backward against the right foot. With both feet extended, toes down, a nail was driven through the arch of each, leaving the knees moderately flexed. Jesus was now crucified.[17]

The situation only *worsened* from this point onward. The medical aspects included much more than blood loss:

> As the arms fatigued, great waves of cramps swept over the muscles, knotting them in deep relentless, throbbing

pain. With these cramps came the inability [of Jesus] to push Himself upward. Hanging by the arms, the pectoral muscles, the large muscles of the chest, were paralyzed and the intercostal muscles, the small muscles between the ribs, were unable to act. Air could be drawn into the lungs, but could not be exhaled. Jesus fought to raise Himself in order to get even one short breath. Finally, the carbon dioxide level increased in the lungs and in the bloodstream, and the cramps partially subsided.[18]

The common method of ending a crucifixion was by breaking the bones of the legs. This prevented the victim from pushing himself upward so he could gasp for air. Rapid suffocation would occur, quickly ending the hours of suffering. According to the Gospel writers, the legs of the two thieves crucified with Jesus were broken, but when the soldiers prepared to perform the same act on Jesus, they saw that it was unnecessary. Most likely the soldiers realized Jesus had not pulled himself up on the cross in order to breathe. He had been hanging downward long enough to assure the soldiers he had already died.

Because no one was intended to survive crucifixions, the bodies of victims were not released to the family until the soldiers were sure that the person was dead. By custom, one of the Roman guards would pierce the body with a sword or lance.[19] In John's account of the crucifixion we read, "One of the soldiers pierced Jesus' side with a spear, bringing a sudden flow of blood and water."[20] The watery fluid came from the sac surrounding the heart, and the blood from the interior of the heart.

This is conclusive evidence that Jesus died—if not by asphyxiation, then certainly because of heart failure. As one article on the issue stated, "This is rather conclusive post-mortem evidence that Jesus died, not the usual crucifixion death by suffocation, but of heart failure due to shock and constriction of the heart by fluid in the pericardium."[21]

## In Their Words

"The major pathophysiologic effect of crucifixion was an interference with normal respirations. Accordingly death resulted primarily from hypovolemic shock and exhaustion asphyxia. Jesus' death was ensured by the thrust of a soldier's spear into his side. Modern medical interpretation of the historical evidence indicates that Jesus was dead when taken down from the cross."

–JOURNAL OF THE AMERICAN MEDICAL ASSOCIATION, 1986; 255:1455-63

Dr. Norm Geisler, who has studied these issues extensively, observes,

> Clearly, the weight of historical and medical evidence indicates that Jesus was dead before the wound to his side was inflicted and supports the traditional view that the spear, thrust between his right ribs, probably perforated not only the right lung but also the pericardium and heart and thereby ensured his death. Accordingly, interpretations based on the assumption that Jesus did not die on the cross appear to be at odds with modern biblical knowledge.[22]

## So What?

Unless you're a medical professional or budding medical student, some of these details may make you sick to your stomach. So what's the big deal about this talk of Jesus *definitely dying* on the cross?

Our discussion here serves two purposes. First, it doesn't make sense to talk about Jesus' resurrection without first answering the questions about how he died. It doesn't matter if the tomb was empty if the emptiness resulted from Jesus walking out of it after a concussion or coma.

Second, it's important to realize that believing Jesus died in the way described by Matthew, Mark, Luke, and John is not just a fairy tale. It is a belief based on an abundance of diverse historical writings. Archaeological expert J.H. Charlesworth summarized the importance of this information best: "It is not a confession of faith to affirm that Jesus died on Golgotha that Friday afternoon; it is a probability obtained by the highest canons of scientific historical research."[23]

Now that we've confirmed Jesus was dead on arrival at the tomb, what about his body, his corpse? Where did it go? Did his friends take it? Was it hidden? Or could Jesus have really walked out...alive?

The Burial of Jesus:

# How Was He
**10** | **Buried?**

*"Between the crucifixion and the resurrection there is
the burial of Jesus. And at first thought it would seem
to be anything but miraculous, a rather mundane and
necessary act with little or no consequence except for
what happens on both ends of it. But that's not the case
at all. The burial of Jesus Christ is as supernatural and
as miraculous in many ways as was His death."*
—DR. JOHN MACARTHUR[1]

In June 2000, ABC aired a two-hour special entitled *The Search for Jesus*. After its release, the owner of a major Christian television network asked me (John) if I would interview some of the world's most respected scholars to provide a Christian perspective on ABC's report. I agreed, and that next year I interviewed scholars from several countries across three continents, including some filming that was done in Israel.

During the process, we interviewed 21 of the top historians, archaeologists, philosophers, and theologians on the life of Jesus. The compilation included over 100 hours of recorded interviews transcribed into 1,500 pages of information. It took 600 hours to research that information and write the script that would be used in the two-hour television special.

The final 40 minutes of this enormous venture were devoted to the central historical facts about the end of Jesus' life. As we look now at the burial of Jesus, I would like to share some of the words these scholars had to say about Jesus' final days on earth.

## The Archaeology of Jesus' Burial

Dr. William Lane Craig introduced the subject by saying, "With respect to...the honorable burial of Jesus, the majority of New Testament scholars who have written on this subject agree that Jesus of Nazareth was buried by Joseph of Arimathea in a tomb."

The Gospel writer Mark provides the early written account of this event:

> It was Preparation Day (that is, the day before the Sabbath). So as evening approached, Joseph of Arimathea, a prominent member of the Council, who was himself waiting for the kingdom of God, went boldly to Pilate and asked for Jesus' body. Pilate was surprised to hear that he was already dead. Summoning the centurion, he asked him if Jesus had already died. When he learned from the centurion that it was so, he gave the body to Joseph. So Joseph bought some linen cloth, took down the body, wrapped it in the linen, and placed it in a tomb cut out of rock. Then he rolled a stone against the entrance of the tomb.[2]

All four Gospels report that Joseph of Arimathea requested permission from Pilate to bury Jesus, and that Jesus' body was laid in a tomb cut out of solid rock. Three of the writers say the tomb was new—that no one had ever been laid in the tomb before. But does this information agree with what archaeologists in Israel have discovered in their investigations?

*Comparing Tombs*

Jewish archaeologist Dr. Gabriel Barkay, considered one of the foremost authorities on tombs in Jerusalem during the first century, shared on this aspect of Jesus' burial. I asked him, "What current archaeological evidence supports the description given in the Gospels about the tomb in which Jesus was buried?"

Dr. Barkley responded, "We have the fact that it was a rich man's tomb. We have, most probably, the allusion to the fact that it was outside the city of Jerusalem. We have the stone found unrolled three days later.

"Altogether we have about a thousand burial caves from the time of Jesus surrounding Jerusalem. The details that we have in the Gospels about the burial of Jesus fit well with the evidence we have in the field."

*Other Theories*

Dr. William Lane Craig, responding to the ABC special *The Search for Jesus,* noted, "I was somewhat amused when ABC said that according to the Gospels, Jesus was laid in the tomb by his mother and his friends. If the story of Jesus' burial was a late-developing legend that accrued over the decades in the early Christian church, that is exactly the sort of pious story that one would expect to find. But that's not what the Gospels say.

"Instead, what the Gospels say is that Jesus of Nazareth was laid in a tomb by this enigmatic figure, Joseph of Arimathea, who appears out of nowhere in the Gospels. Contrary to expectation, he gives Jesus of Nazareth an honorable burial in a tomb. Moreover, Mark tells us that this man was a member of the Sanhedrin, the very council that had just condemned Jesus to be crucified. Then Joseph singles out Jesus among the trio of men who had been crucified for special care by giving him an honorable burial in a tomb rather than allowing the body to simply be dispatched into a common grave reserved for criminals. This is extraordinary and requires some sort of explanation."

In spite of the evidence for the honorable burial of Jesus, John Dominic Crossan said this during the ABC special: "After Jesus died on a cross, he was thrown on a trash heap and chewed up by wild dogs."

When I asked Dr. Habermas about this, he said, "I could say for the moment that it's interesting that virtually none of his friends have followed him in claiming this. That doesn't prove anything, but maybe it's a hint that the data is not in his favor. One thing I would say is that we are devoid of a *single fact* that says that happened to Jesus. We have a lot of reasons to think that he was buried and that the tomb in which he was buried was empty—but nothing, not any fact, that says he was thrown into a common grave."

Dr. William Lane Craig agrees. "The historical credibility of the burial account of Jesus by Joseph of Arimathea leaves skeptical critics in an extremely awkward position. If Jesus was in fact buried by a Jewish Sanhedrist in Jerusalem, as the Gospels claim, that means that the location of Jesus' tomb was known to both Jews and Christians alike. But in that case, it's impossible to imagine how a movement founded on belief in the resurrection of a dead man who had been publicly executed in Jerusalem could arise and flourish in the face of a tomb containing his corpse. So those scholars who want to deny such things as the empty tomb and the resurrection appearances also find themselves forced to deny the fact of the honorable burial of Jesus, even though this is one of the earliest and best attested facts about the historical Jesus that we have. It's extremely awkward for them."

## The Location of Jesus' Burial

One of the most impressive stops during my time of research for this program was at the Church of the Holy Sepulcher in Jerusalem. According to archaeologists, it traditionally marks the actual site of the tomb in which Jesus was buried by Joseph of Arimathea.

While standing in front of this revered site, I spoke with Dr. Magen Broshi, a respected Jewish archaeologist and scholar on the second temple period. He is the former curator of the Shrine of the Book Museum in Jerusalem, in which the Dead Sea scrolls are housed. When asked about whether he thought this was the location where Jesus had been buried, he answered, based on his research, "There is high probability. A very high probability."

And he should know. Dr. Broshi was asked to conduct the excavation at the Church of the Holy Sepulcher for a rather unusual reason. According to the interview, he shared that "they invited me to participate in the dig. What was very important for them was that I was considered an infidel. I wasn't a Christian. They didn't want Catholics. They didn't want Greek Orthodox. They wanted somebody who was absolutely neutral and I was that person."

In other words, Dr. Broshi did not come to his conclusion with a personal bias to prove Jesus was or was not buried there. Yet the evidence he found while excavating at the Church of the Holy Sepulcher led him to defend it as the most reasonable place for the burial of Jesus.

When I asked him why, he revealed, "Two reasons. One is that the tradition should be trusted. It was too important to be forgotten, and there was a Christian community in and around Jerusalem that would have carried it on and handed it down from one generation to the other. The second reason is that this area was a graveyard at the time of Jesus, and there are several graves around here now. There were more, but they were obliterated by later building activity."

So far, our experts have noted that the location of Jesus' burial fits tradition and the surrounding evidence, along with the historical fact that there is no comparable alternative theory. While these insights were helpful, what Dr. Broshi shared later provided even more compelling information that is consistent with what the Gospels say about Jesus' burial.

## The Burial Stone

All four Gospel accounts mention a stone that was rolled against the entrance to the tomb. Mark said that it was a "very large" stone.[3] So I asked Dr. Broshi about it, saying, "The Gospel accounts talk about a stone that was rolled in front of the tomb. Does that make sense to you?"

"Why not? We found it."

"You found it?" I clarified.

"Not here, but in many other places, the rolling stone. Sometimes they weigh more than a regular car. But being round, you know, you can roll it."

"Why did they place a stone in front of the tomb?"

"To keep the robbers out; to keep animals away from the tombs."

According to Dr. Broshi, the New Testament description of Jesus' burial, which included a large stone over the tomb entrance, accurately fits the burial practices of first-century Jerusalem.

## The Burial Process

The Gospel writers indicate that Jesus' burial was a hurried process. Because the Jewish Sabbath was approaching, the body needed to be in the tomb by nightfall. Nicodemus brought a mixture of spices for the burial of Jesus' body.[4] From the extraordinary amount he brought we can calculate Nicodemus was an affluent, upper-class citizen. From what we can tell, he brought the equivalent of about 75 pounds (34 kg) of spices.[5] These spices were used to prepare Jesus' body for burial. Then his body was wrapped with linen strips like bandages and covered with a large sheet called a shroud. He was then laid in a new tomb owned by Joseph, and a large rock was rolled in front of the entrance to contain the body's odor and prevent possible entry by animals or thieves.

## Moving Forward

What is significant about these details is that they once again confirm we are definitely talking about a dead body. The Gospel writers then record that on Sunday, Jesus' female followers came with more spices with which to anoint the body of their dead friend.[6] In doing so, they had no expectation that he would be alive. Who would argue that a crucified man, pronounced dead at the cross, and bound like a mummy with 75 pounds of spices *could* wake up and decide to get out? If Jesus managed to do that, then we're talking about an act at the level of the supernatural—the very thing those arguing against Jesus' resurrection vehemently oppose.

Yet this type of questioning is important to consider and leads us to another historical issue to discuss. Was Jesus' tomb really found empty on the third day? If so, where did his body go? Our next chapter deals with the details of this very controversy.

The Empty Tomb of Jesus:

# Where Did His Body Go?

**11**

---

*"Conflicting traditions [to the empty tomb story] nowhere appear, even in Jewish polemic."*

—DR. WILLIAM LANE CRAIG[1]

*"[The resurrection story] could not have been maintained in Jerusalem for a single day, for a single hour, if the emptiness of the tomb had not been established...."*

—DR. PAUL ALTHAUS[2]

Where did the body of Jesus disappear to? If he died and was buried, what happened to him?

This is the third major fact historians must evaluate—the empty tomb (the first two facts are his death and his burial). All the early sources report that Jesus' tomb was found empty—first by women, then by his disciples, and finally, by the Jewish leaders themselves. In a 2001 interview, Dr. William Lane Craig shared that "today, the majority of scholars who have written on this subject agree that the tomb of Jesus was probably found empty by a group of his female followers early on Sunday morning. That represents the historical core of the empty tomb narrative as we find it in Mark."[3]

According to Dr. Gary Habermas, "The empty tomb is preached

very early. You have Paul in 1 Corinthians 15 saying Jesus died, he was buried, and what went down is what came out, and what came out is what appeared. First Corinthians is already early, about 25 years after the cross. But then the creedal passage that he reports from 1 Corinthians 15 is earlier still. In Galatians, Paul has apostolic confirmation of his message about the resurrection events. These come from Peter and James in Galatians 1 and from Peter, James, and John in Galatians 2. This testimony was given to Paul *within five years of Jesus' resurrection* from those preaching since day one. So you have this intricate, interwoven, and accredited eyewitness messenger with an early book, with an even earlier creed. Ultimately, it's teaching our fact here in question—the empty tomb."

## The Response of the Jewish Leaders

In addition to the supporting historical sources written by the followers of Jesus, we find that the Jewish leadership of that day confirmed the early story of the empty tomb of Jesus. Dr. William Lane Craig notes that "the earliest Jewish response to the proclamation of the resurrection was not to point to the occupied tomb, but rather, to say that the disciples had stolen the body. It was itself an attempt to explain away why the body was missing.

"What we have here is evidence from the very enemies of the earliest Christian movement in favor of the empty tomb, evidence that is simply top drawer, because it comes not from the Christians, but from the very opponents of the early Christian movement." The most common alternatives today continue to suggest some form of Jesus' followers removing his body and then announcing he was alive again.

Yet according to Dr. Craig, within academic circles, "Nobody says that anymore. That theory has been completely abandoned since the early 1800s. No responsible scholar holds to such a thing."

I (John) was surprised to hear this report. I followed up by asking Dr. Gary Habermas, "But why have scholars concluded the disciples did not steal Jesus' body? Why have they abandoned the theory that Jesus didn't die on the cross or that he just fainted?"

Habermas then traced this controversy back to its roots. "In his major work in 1835 in *The Life of Jesus* [David Friedrich] Strauss said the swoon theory is not going to work and the problem was this: It is self-contradictory. What you have from the 'swoon' is a living Jesus but not a resurrected Jesus.

"Here's how it works. Jesus should have died on the cross, but he didn't. He should have died in the tomb. He didn't. He certainly can't roll the stone away. No problem. He did. Now, Strauss didn't believe there was a guard, but for those who believe guards were out there, he works his way through the guards. But here's the problem for Strauss. Jesus comes to where the disciples are and knocks on the door.

"What's this man going to look like? He's a *human* Jesus. He's been crucified. He's worked the wounds open again. He's bleeding from the scalp. His hair hasn't even been washed. You have sweat and blood, and he's worked the side open again. And he's hunched over, he's limping, he's pale. One problem Strauss had with the swoon theory is that you get a Jesus who is alive, but you don't get a Jesus who is *raised*.

"Now, Strauss does not believe in the resurrection, but he knows the disciples did. And the swoon doesn't get you from A to B. You get this kind of Jesus: 'Lord, come on in. Get a chair. Get a pail of water. Call the doctor.' The problem is that the swoon can't account for the experiences that the disciples had that they thought were appearances of the risen Jesus."

## Questioning the Disciples About the Empty Tomb

This brings us to the third major historical fact that must be accounted for: On the Sunday following Jesus' crucifixion, the tomb of Jesus was found empty by his followers. Our remaining conversation in this chapter will shift from talk about Jesus' death to a dialogue concerning possible opportunities his followers may have had to reclaim his body. If Jesus' friends did take him away from his burial site, several questions would have required a credible answer. We'll consider four of the most important requirements the followers of Jesus would have had to fulfill to steal his dead body and proclaim Jesus had come back to life from the dead.

### Did They Have a Motive?

The friends and followers of Jesus taught that he had come back to life. Were they lying? If so, what would be their motivation? Was dissatisfaction with the Roman government enough? Not likely.

Jesus, according to his followers, modeled values of love, truth, and selfless living. Would it make sense for his closest associates to completely contradict their leader? According to one article on the subject:

> At best all anyone can do is guess about what the disciples *may* have been thinking or what *might* have motivated them to devise an elaborate deception. Guessing is all that can be done. But we would need to ask if any proposed motives of the disciples could be harmonized with the facts of their preaching and teaching about truth, long-suffering, patience, kindness, and love. No one can read their hearts or their minds and insert into a scenario 2,000 years old the motivations of people long gone. It is best to simply let the facts speak for themselves. They lived, suffered, proclaimed, and died for the truth of the resurrection.[4]

Regardless of what their motive was to teach about a risen Jesus, we can see that such a change would be in complete contrast with what Jesus had taught them over the previous three years. Yet their teaching had tremendous impact.

Even according to the best of today's research, the most likely historical scenario is that the tomb was empty. The question at hand among scholars today is this: How did it happen?

### Did They Have a Plan?

No matter what theory we believe, we would all likely agree that Jesus' followers would have needed some kind of plan to pull off an operation for stealing the body of Jesus. Why? According to history, the tomb was guarded by a group of Roman soldiers. If the disciples were to accomplish such a task, they would have had to bribe or kill the guards, move the stone, and then move the body to another location. This would certainly require the help of several people.

And the consequences? If caught, those involved would likely be killed in the process. If captured, they might suffer death by crucifixion as well. But does this match what we know about the behavior of those disheartened followers after Jesus' brutal death?

According to the Gospel accounts, Jesus' friends were behind locked doors, fearful for their own lives. That they continued to mourn the death of Jesus is evident because the women who went to visit the tomb on Sunday morning had spices intended for use on Jesus' dead body.

But suppose for a moment Jesus' followers *did* obtain the body. Certainly they would have needed to dispose of the body in some way to prevent someone from finding his corpse as evidence against them. Would they burn it? Not if they observed Jewish law. Would they rebury it? Certainly Jewish custom required this, but this would mean that men who had given up their careers and social status to follow a man who taught honesty and integrity were now rebels of both Roman and Jewish laws. Such a scenario would be inconsistent.

Consider this thought: What do you suppose would happen if Jesus' followers had stolen his body yet continued to announce Jesus was alive? First, there would have been persecution from the Jewish religious leaders. In fact, this did occur. Ten of the eleven remaining disciples died as martyrs for their faith. The only exception was John, who was banished to the island of Patmos near the end of his life. Usually if deception is involved, at least one person would "crack" in the process and confess to what had been done. And history would certainly have recorded such.

### Did They Have the Resources?

Another factor to consider is whether the followers of Jesus would have had the resources to obtain Jesus' body. The only ways to get past the Roman guards were to either obtain the weapons to overpower the guards or to obtain enough money to bribe the guards. Both options have severe weaknesses.

Consider the idea that Jesus' followers would gather weapons and attempt to take down a group of Roman guards. The night of Jesus' arrest, Jesus asked his disciples if they had *any* weapons. They found two—two weapons for 12 disciples and Jesus. They had only two short swords, nothing that could be used against a battalion of armed troops.

Most of Jesus' disciples were fishermen by trade. They were not trained in martial arts or the modern weaponry of the day. They did not have backgrounds as soldiers, except possibly Simon the Zealot. To obtain the weapons they would have needed to either make them (highly unlikely) or buy them.

Speaking of buying, what about the idea of Jesus' followers paying off the guards for his body? How likely would this option have been? There are a couple of factors to consider: First, where would Jesus' followers have been able to obtain a large sum of money within three days of his death? The only wealthy ones among them were Joseph of Arimathea, who had provided the tomb, and Nicodemus, who assisted in burying Jesus. Joseph, a member of the Jewish court that had condemned Jesus, had probably already risked his reputation when he asked for the body. The chances of Joseph stealing the body from his own tomb three days later? Very slim.

Second, even if Jesus' followers somehow obtained a windfall of money to pay off the guards, would the guards have taken it? Consider the consequences. If the Roman soldiers had lost the body, they would have paid for it with their lives. To phrase it in our terms, would you rather have ten million dollars and die tomorrow, or have no money and enjoy the rest of your life? To the Roman soldiers, this was the predicament.

The New Testament confirms for us that there were grave consequences for Roman soldiers who lost a person whom they were guarding. In Acts 16:25-30, when Paul was in prison, there was an earthquake that opened the cell doors that would have allowed the prisoners to escape. When the officer in charge saw this, he prepared to commit suicide. Why? He knew his life would be taken if his prisoners escaped. And in Acts 12:18-19, we find Peter in prison for his faith. In this passage we read that Herod specifically ordered the guards to be executed if Peter escaped.

Interestingly, in the Gospel accounts, we read it was the *Jewish religious leaders* who paid money to the guards to say that the disciples had stolen the body *after* the tomb had been found empty. We are told:

> Now while they were on their way, some of the guard came into the city and reported to the chief priests all that had happened. And when they had assembled with the elders and consulted together, they gave a large sum of money to the soldiers, and said, "You are to say, 'His disciples came by night and stole Him away while we were asleep.' And if this should come to the governor's ears, we will win him over and keep you out of trouble." And they took the money and did as they had been instructed; and this story was widely spread among the Jews, and is to this day.[5]

We are never told in the Gospels what happened to the guards at the tomb.

"I claim to be a historian. My approach to classics is historical. And I tell you that the evidence for the life, the death, and the resurrection of Christ is better authenticated than most of the facts of ancient history."

—**DR. E.M. BLAIKLOCK,** PROFESSOR OF CLASSICS, AUCKLAND UNIVERSITY[6]

### Did They Have the Connections?

By *connections* we mean this: Did the disciples have influence over enough people to encourage hundreds of people to lie about seeing Jesus alive again? How could they have been able to convince so many to speak out about a person who had just been put to death by the government? These people's jobs, social status, and families would all have been at stake.

Consider the sheer numbers. In 1 Corinthians 15, which the

apostle Paul wrote just over 20 years later, he said that over 500 people had seen Jesus alive after his resurrection, most of whom were still alive at the time of Paul's writing. Is it plausible to think that 500 people could be influenced by a handful of men to lie about such a well-known event? Extremely unlikely. Such a theory requires a tremendous jump of faith. This being the situation, we are left to choose the most likely option: that Jesus really did rise from the dead.

> "Therefore, as a historian I am forced to say that two things must have happened: One, they certainly had sightings of Jesus; but two, they really knew the tomb was empty. Either of those without the other, and they would have had easy explanations: Empty tomb—someone has stolen the body. Visions—it's just one of those visions. They happen, and it doesn't mean he's not dead. But the fact is, they said, 'He isn't dead anymore.' Resurrection is not a way of redescribing death in a rather more hopeful fashion. It's a way of overthrowing death. That's at the center of the New Testament."
>
> —DR. N.T. WRIGHT[7]

## What Now?

Jesus was not missing in action. His body was buried and guarded, yet it disappeared. The historical evidence shows that Jesus was crucified on a cross, his body was laid in a tomb cut out of solid rock, and three days later, that tomb was found empty.

What happened to Jesus' body? And what turned the disciples from cowards to having the courage to proclaim that "God has raised this Jesus to life, and we are all witnesses of the fact"?[8] These are the questions we will tackle in our next chapter.

The Appearances of Jesus:

# Did People Really See Him Alive after His Death?

**12**

*"Don't start by saying, 'Did he really walk on water?'
Don't start by saying, 'Was he really born of a virgin?' If
you start with those questions, you go round and round
in circles and you never get anywhere. Start by saying,
'How do you explain the rise of early Christianity?' And
if it comes back and says, 'It was Jesus' resurrection,'
then you're going to have to hold your mind open to the
fact that in the world, as Shakespeare said, 'There are
more things in heaven and earth than are dreamed of
in your philosophy.'"*

—DR. N.T. WRIGHT, CANON THEOLOGIAN OF WESTMINSTER ABBEY[1]

Elvis is alive!" claims *The Weekly World News.*[2] Many believe they
have seen Elvis Presley in recent years. There is even an Elvis
Sighting Society based at the Newport Restaurant in Ottawa,
Canada.[3] Yet the vast majority of people surveyed do not believe
these sightings are for real.

What makes the claims of Jesus sightings any different from
claims of Elvis sightings? Could they be just as much of a hoax?

According to Dr. William Lane Craig, "The fourth fundamental fact that any responsible historical hypothesis has to account for in explaining the fate of Jesus of Nazareth is the fact that after his death different individuals and groups of people claimed to have seen Jesus of Nazareth alive from the dead on different occasions and under varying circumstances. Now, this general fact is one that is universally acknowledged today among New Testament critics."

But the New Testament writings also teach that Jesus' followers fled in despair when he was crucified and they knew he had died and was buried in a tomb. After Jesus' death, they hid themselves in a locked room. What convinced the disciples that Jesus was no longer dead, but had risen from the grave?

## A Big Enough X

New Testament professor Dr. Ben Witherington provides an insightful perspective on this issue. In my (John's) interview with him, he stated, "In terms of the psychological profile of the disciples, if we believe it is true that they denied, deserted, and betrayed Jesus, that they had given him up for lost when he died on the cross, psychologically something significant had to have happened to change all of their minds about this particular issue after the crucifixion of Jesus. Remember, no early Jews were looking for a crucified Messiah. If you wanted to stop the rumor that Jesus was Messiah, get him crucified. That would prove that he was cursed, not blessed by God.

"So here they are, completely shattered, their world has been turned upside down, they've spent the last three years of their lives, apparently for nothing, following Jesus. *What was going to change that opinion?* Something from outside of themselves had to impact them like a sledgehammer, hitting them over the head to change their mind about the fact that Jesus was dead and gone.

"Something dramatic had to have happened. You need to posit an X big enough between the death of Jesus and the birth of the early church to explain the connection. If you don't posit an X big enough, then you haven't explained the historical connection."

## How Many Eyewitnesses?

How many people claimed to have seen Jesus alive after the crucifixion? According to Habermas, the key list is in 1 Corinthians 15. "In that list you have individuals, including leaders of the church. Paul starts with Peter, ends with himself, and in the middle has James, the brother of Jesus—three key individuals who saw the risen Jesus.

### How Many People Saw Jesus Alive?

- 3 women

- 2 men on the Emmaus road

- 11 disciples

- 500 people at one time

- James, brother of Jesus

- Paul (after the 40 postresurrection days)

**TOTAL:** 518, unless some of the 500 were the same as other sightings. Luke also alludes that there may have been *additional* sightings.

"But you also have *groups,* and that's very important for ascertaining some evidence for these appearances. You have the Twelve—a group he calls 'all the apostles'—and you have more than 500 people, most of whom were still alive when Paul wrote these words.

"Now, when you go to the Gospels, I think also with good grounds we have, for example, the women. You have several women at the tomb and probably Mary Magdalene alone as she returns. So you see them sighting Jesus as well as the empty tomb. But in those days, if you're going to put your best foot forward, you do not use women because they can't go to a law court. You're not going to impress people in first-century Palestine. By far the best reason for starting with the women and secondarily with Mary is very simple—they saw the risen Jesus.

"Now, the Gospels also tell us about a long walk two men had with a visitor on the way to Emmaus. These two men walk and talk for miles with this visitor before they realize he is Jesus. Then Jesus made multiple appearances to varying groups of the disciples. John 20 documents an appearance before all the disciples except, of course, Judas and Thomas. A week later is a second appearance—this time with Thomas on hand. So you have a number of sightings, which include men and women, individuals and groups. You have Jesus indoors, outdoors, sitting, standing, fishing, making a shore lunch, and walking with others."

## What Did They See?

These appearances, however, are looked at very differently by various scholars today. What did these people really see? Did they see Jesus in his physical body or in some kind of a vision?

*A Physical Appearance*

Dr. Witherington shares that "most scholars would certainly say that the disciples believed that they saw Jesus, and many of them would want to just leave it there and say, 'Okay, it was subjective phenomenon that happened here.'

"But if you interpret the Gospel documents about the resurrection appearances of the risen Lord, and you interpret the Pauline evidence, and the rest of the New Testament evidence, they were claiming far more than that. They were claiming to actually have a *physical encounter* with Jesus after his death—that he ate, was tangible, could be touched, and that he was still moving in space and time as a real person. They were claiming more than just having had a vision of Jesus."

Academic researchers have used different words to describe what they think the disciples saw. Some claim the disciples saw an ordinary appearance of Jesus. This is the traditional view that Jesus was literally, physically present with them. He ate with them and invited them to touch him. In the words of Dr. William Lane Craig, "If there had been people there with audio recorders and cameras, they would have had photographic and audio images of Jesus appearing in the Upper Room. That would be an ordinary appearance."

## More Than a Vision

Other scholars use the word *vision* to describe what they think the disciples saw. A *vision* is defined as seeing an object in the mind without the use or help of the five senses. Further, there are two kinds of visions: truthful visions and false visions. An example of a true vision would be a revelation given by God to a person.

As Dr. William Lane Craig defines, "A truthful vision would be what Stephen saw when he was stoned. He looked up and saw the heavens opened and he said, 'I see heaven open and the Son of Man, standing at the right hand of God.' [4] But those persecuting Stephen saw nothing at all. They didn't perceive anything and killed him. What Stephen saw was a truthful vision, a God-induced visionary seeing of the exalted Christ."

Yet there are also false visions. An example would be a person who gets drunk and sees a pink elephant. The person might really "see" the pink elephant, but it is a hallucination, purely a figment of the person's own imagination. This is what scholars usually mean when they admit that the disciples "saw" Jesus. They say the disciples merely had some kind of vision rather than saw a literal, physical appearance of Jesus. This raises a key question: Did the disciples know the difference between a real physical appearance of Jesus and a vision of Jesus in their minds?

Dr. Craig observes, "It's interesting that the New Testament draws a clear distinction between *appearances* of Christ and *visions* of Christ. The appearances of the risen Christ were to a limited circle and soon ceased. But visions of the exalted Christ continued in the New Testament church. Paul experienced such when he was praying in the temple in Jerusalem. Stephen saw a vision of Christ at his stoning. In the book of Revelation, John has a vision of the throne room of God. So the visions in the church were something that did not cease, yet these were distinct from a resurrection appearance."

### More Than a Hallucination

In an interview with Dr. Habermas, I (John) asked, "What's wrong with the hallucination theory?" I knew he would have strong thoughts on this issue, but I was surprised at the staggering amount of information included in his response. Habermas specifically noted four problems with the suggestion that Jesus' followers were hallucinating when they claimed to see Jesus alive again:

> **Problem #1:** *Different people in groups do not see the same hallucination.* A hallucination is something you believe so firmly that you *invent* the mental picture. Two different people cannot share a hallucination any more than two different people can share a dream.

> **Problem #2:** *The disciples were not expecting to see Jesus alive again.* It's granted by everybody, both from scripture and from psychology, that you can't have exuberant, expecting disciples after the calamity that took place at the cross. The disciples were not in the right frame of mind to have such positive hallucinations.

> **Problem #3:** *Too many people, times, and places.* To believe that every one of these people manufactured a private, individual hallucination that supposedly matched many other hallucinations is unrealistic.

> **Problem #4:** *The empty tomb.* If the people were merely hallucinating, the tomb wouldn't have been empty. The religious leaders could have easily proven these hallucinations wrong by digging up Jesus' body and placing it on public display. They didn't because it wasn't there.

Ultimately, neither visions nor hallucinations explain the incredible transformation that took place in the disciples. According to Dr. Craig, "Given the typical Jewish mentality about beliefs in the afterlife, they would have believed that Jesus would have gone to Abraham's bosom, to paradise, where the souls of the righteous dead would be with God until the resurrection at the end of the world. If they had hallucinated visions of Jesus, they would have projected visions of him as exalted in heaven, where God had taken him up until the resurrection at the end of the world.

"But that, at most, would have led them to the glorification of Jesus in heaven, not his literal resurrection from the dead. For the Jew, the resurrection was an event that took place in space and time, in history, and therefore something more is needed than just hallucinations to explain why the disciples came to believe in the resurrection of Jesus rather than merely his translation into heaven."

## The Sightings

Who were the individuals who claimed to see Jesus alive after his death? As we thumb through the pages of the New Testament, we find 12 distinct encounters recorded between Jesus and individuals who saw him after his resurrection.

### *Jesus Sighting #1*

The first Jesus sighting occurred early Sunday morning: "When Jesus rose early on the first day of the week, he appeared first to Mary Magdalene, out of whom he had driven seven demons."[5]

The full story reveals that Mary's first reaction was grief. This is understandable for someone who had lost a loved one. When she saw a person near the tomb, she thought it was a gardener, not Jesus. It was only when Jesus spoke to her that she recognized his voice. She clung to him and then ran to tell the others.

Does anything in this story seem out of place? Only a man who was dead and is now alive. That's the point: Jesus alive again is the one supernatural, stunning highlight of the account.

### *Jesus Sighting #2*

Matthew's biography of Jesus tells what happened as the three women—Mary Magdalene, Mary mother of James, and Salome[6] left the tomb to tell the disciples that it was empty:

Suddenly Jesus met them. "Greetings," he said. They came to him, clasped his feet and worshiped him. Then Jesus said to them, "Do not be afraid. Go and tell my brothers to go to Galilee; there they will see me."[7]

## A Woman First?

In first-century Jewish culture, a female's testimony was not given the same weight as a testimony from a man. If Jesus' followers were fabricating a story about the resurrection, it is highly unlikely that they would have had Jesus sighted by a woman first.

Here we find not only Mary but two additional women encountering the risen Jesus. This was significant in Jewish culture because all matters required two or three witnesses to be confirmed as a fact. Their response? They rushed back to the home where the disciples were staying to tell the amazing news. Again, everything in this account is normal except for the fact Jesus was spotted alive (see Appendix B for further details of this account).[8]

### Jesus Sighting #3

The next Jesus sighting involves one of the most significant postresurrection stories. As two men travel the road from Jerusalem to Emmaus, Jesus begins walking with them, asking questions and sharing his interpretations of the Jewish prophecies regarding the Messiah. They later stop to share a meal together. Not until then do the men realize it is Jesus who is with them.[9]

Why is this sighting significant? First, as far as we can reconstruct, these are the first men Jesus appeared to (though Sighting #4 may have occurred before Sighting #3). This would affirm the testimony given earlier by the three women.

Second, we realize that Jesus' body must somehow now be different. Why? The two men did not recognize him for some time. Also, Jesus is now making extremely speedy travel time as he goes from the tomb to the Emmaus road, then to Peter back in Jerusalem. He also has the ability to suddenly disappear—when the two men recognized him, Jesus vanished from their sight.

*Jesus Sighting #4*

The two men walking to Emmaus went back to Jerusalem to find the disciples. "There they found the Eleven and those with them, assembled together and saying, 'It is true! The Lord has risen and has appeared to Simon.'"[10] Apparently somewhere between the time Jesus disappeared from dinner to the time these two men relayed their story to the 11 disciples, Jesus had also appeared to Peter.

Paul notes this again in 1 Corinthians 15:5: "[Jesus] was raised on the third day according to the Scriptures, and...he appeared to Peter."[11] Peter would later stand in the streets of Jerusalem on the crowded holiday of Pentecost to call thousands to follow this risen Jesus. By this point we have four sightings by a total of six people—three women, three men—all before nightfall on the day of Jesus' resurrection.

*Jesus Sighting #5*

The next Jesus sighting was not by one or two or even three people, but by ten of the disciples, the two men returning from Emmaus, and probably the women and perhaps additional followers. Instead of seven people encountering a resurrected Jesus, we now have at least a dozen men plus women and any others who were in the room at the time.[12]

First, the people were scared and thought they were seeing a ghost. Jesus told them to look at his hands and feet, but still they did not believe what they were experiencing. Jesus then ate food in their midst, and everyone finally realized this Jesus before them was not a spirit but a real resurrected body!

The disciples had seen Jesus bring two people back to life over the course of his ministry, but apparently could not even fathom Jesus himself coming back to life. Luke records these men as being thoroughly stunned.

*Jesus Sighting #6*

The disciple Thomas happened to be absent at Sighting #5, and when the other disciples told Thomas what had happened, he didn't believe them. His response gave rise to the name Doubting Thomas:

> Now Thomas (called Didymus), one of the Twelve, was not with the disciples when Jesus came. So the other disciples told him, "We have seen the Lord!"
>
> But he said to them, "Unless I see the nail marks in his hands and put my finger where the nails were, and put my hand into his side, I will not believe it."[13]

For an entire week, Thomas must have wrestled with the arguments of over a dozen people, including his closest friends, who attempted to convince him that Jesus really was alive. *But dead people don't come back to life on their own,* thought Thomas. *It just wasn't possible—or was it?*

> A week later [Jesus'] disciples were in the house again, and Thomas was with them. Though the doors were locked, Jesus came and stood among them and said, "Peace be with you!" Then he said to Thomas, "Put your finger here; see my hands. Reach out your hand and put it into my side. Stop doubting and believe."
>
> Thomas said to him, "My Lord and my God!"[14]

The tomb could not contain Jesus, so we should not be surprised to discover him finding his way past a locked door. Thomas apparently didn't need any more convincing, either. His short and profound realization was that Jesus had proven himself to be the Lord, the Messiah, *his* God.

*Jesus Sighting #7*

The seventh sighting of Jesus, interestingly, took place with seven of his disciples. In John 21, we read that over half of the remaining disciples had taken an all-night fishing trip on the Sea of Galilee. This would not have been out of the ordinary because many of these men were fishermen by trade and would have likely needed some food or a means to purchase, through exchange, other goods they needed. The *unordinary* part of this account was the guy standing on the shore:

> Early in the morning, Jesus stood on the shore, but the disciples did not realize that it was Jesus. He called out to them, "Friends, haven't you any fish?"
>
> "No," they answered.
>
> He said, "Throw your net on the right side of the boat and you will find some." When they did, they were unable to haul the net in because of the large number of fish.
>
> Then the disciple whom Jesus loved said to Peter, "It is the Lord!"[15]

How did the disciples know it was Jesus? There is a connection here to Peter's first encounter with Jesus. In Luke 5, after the disciples went fishing all night without a catch, Jesus told Peter to cast his net into the water. When he did, the disciples caught so many fish that the nets began to break. Following this miracle, Jesus called Peter to be his disciple.

The incident in Luke 5 enabled the disciples, in John 21, to realize the man on the shore was Jesus. Seven of the disciples saw this, so we're not relying here on the claim of just one or two individuals.

### Jesus Sighting #8

Paul later writes that over 500 people saw the resurrected Jesus at one time: "After that, he appeared to more than five hundred of the brothers at the same time, most of whom are still living, though some have fallen asleep."[16]

Why was this of great significance? This sighting was seen by far more than Jesus' core group of followers. If only Jesus' close friends said he was alive, it would be much easier to dismiss them. But with *hundreds* of witnesses who could vouch for what had happened, how could anyone reading Paul's letter not seriously consider that Jesus was really alive?

For some who study about the resurrected Jesus, this solitary verse stands as a defining mark: "If Christ had not been resurrected and then seen by many people (at least over 500 people) the Christian religion never would have made it past the first century."[17] Any other explanation fails to explain the motivational power behind the spread of early Christianity from the first century to today.

### Did You Know...

...that if each of those 500 eyewitnesses were to testify for only six minutes about seeing the risen Jesus, including time for cross-examination, you would have an amazing 50 hours of firsthand testimony? Add to this the testimonies of many other eyewitnesses, and you would well have the largest and most lopsided trial in history.

*Jesus Sighting #9*

In the same chapter, Paul tells us, "Then [Jesus] appeared to James."[18] James was known as the brother of Jesus,[19] leader of the Jerusalem church,[20] and author of the New Testament book of James. Prior to this experience with the risen Jesus, he was portrayed as skeptical of his brother's actions.[21] However, after this face-to-face moment with the resurrected Jesus, he is from then on seen as a proponent and leader of the early Christian movement.[22]

According to Dr. Darrell Bock, "James didn't believe it for a long time and, I think, struggled with it. A turning point for him was the resurrection. I think that [Jesus' family] expected a messianic figure, and then when Jesus said, 'Well, not just Messiah. Look at what I'm doing. Look at the authority that I have,' that made them a little nervous. There was a point at which I think they wrestled with, 'Is that really right?'

"Interestingly enough, John the Baptist went through the same struggle. John questioned Jesus from prison. This indicates there was something about Jesus' ministry that didn't quite fit what John the Baptist was expecting. So he needed some reassurance. Jesus gave that reassurance: 'Look and see what I'm doing. Look what God is doing through me. There's the answer to your question.'"[23]

The significance of this Jesus sighting is that a blood relative of Jesus had turned from skepticism to faith, from rejecting the Jesus movement to leading it. What would cause such a dramatic change? According to Paul, it was Jesus coming back to life.

*Jesus Sighting #10*

Once again the 11 disciples spotted Jesus, this time on a mountain in Galilee: "Then the eleven disciples went to Galilee, to the mountain where Jesus had told them to go. When they saw him, they worshiped him."[24]

During this sighting, Jesus gave a charge to his followers: "Go and make disciples of all nations, baptizing them in the name of the Father and of the Son and of the Holy Spirit, and teaching them to obey everything I have commanded you."[25] The resurrection of Jesus was not intended to be kept a secret. The disciples were to communicate this message to Jews and Gentiles worldwide.

*Jesus Sighting #11*

The final Jesus sighting, which involved the core group of disciples, occurred just before Jesus went back to heaven:

> When he had led them out to the vicinity of Bethany, he lifted up his hands and blessed them. While he was blessing them, he left them and was taken up into heaven. Then they worshiped him and returned to Jerusalem with great joy. And they stayed continually at the temple, praising God.[26]

As was the case with many of the Jewish patriarchs, Jesus ended his earthly life by blessing those closest to him. Then Jesus ascended into the sky in a final departure from his core followers.

Why is this important? There are several reasons, but most important is that we have an end point to the 40 days Jesus appeared to people after his resurrection. Ten days later, Peter preaches in Jerusalem during the Pentecost holiday, and the church is off and running with over 3,000 joining its movement.

### Where Did Jesus Go?

The Christian doctrine of the ascension holds that Jesus physically ascended to heaven in the presence of his disciples following his resurrection. It is narrated in Mark 16:19, Luke 24:50-51, and Acts 1:9-11. It is affirmed by Christian history in the Apostles' Creed and Nicene Creed.[27]

*Jesus Sighting #12*

A couple years later, a zealous Jewish religious leader named Saul was arresting those who followed Jesus. He even stood by in approval of Stephen's death as the first Christian martyr.[28] But Luke tells us in Acts 9 that Saul physically saw Jesus while walking to Damascus. Soon baptized as a Christian, Saul became known as Paul and began Christianity's major spread throughout the Roman Empire.

In his first letter to the Corinthians, Paul briefly described this Jesus sighting: "Last of all he appeared to me also, as to one abnormally born."[29] Paul personally acknowledged that his sighting of Jesus was not normal, but that God used it to change his life for the good of telling others of the resurrection.

## But Wait, There's More!

In addition to the above 12 sightings, Luke tells us that "after his suffering, [Jesus] showed himself to these men and gave many convincing proofs that he was alive. He appeared to them over a period of forty days and spoke about the kingdom of God."[30] While the New Testament writers mentioned 12 distinct sightings, there may have been even more.

The ultimate question with regard to all these sightings is this: What difference do they make? One significant answer is that if Jesus was indeed resurrected and is indeed God's Son, then we now have some serious decisions to make. Do we keep living life "as is," or do we need to evaluate what Jesus says about doing life? In the next chapter, you'll have the opportunity to see for yourself how Jesus' first followers lived in response to his resurrection. As you do so, you'll find that their response to the resurrected Jesus was a very big deal. It changed every aspect of their lives—which is also true about Jesus' followers today.

The Followers of Jesus:

# Did His Friends Believe He Was Alive?

13

*"It's clear and undeniable that the earliest disciples were transformed as a result. They did not go back to fishing and tax collecting. They turned the world upside down."*

—DR. GARY HABERMAS, ON *THE JOHN ANKERBERG SHOW*[1]

*"People will die for their religious beliefs if they sincerely believe they're true, but people won't die for their religious beliefs if they know their beliefs are false."*

—LEE STROBEL, IN *THE CASE FOR CHRIST*[2]

It's one thing to believe in something. It's an entirely different thing to die for your beliefs. As Lee Strobel states in the above quote, some individuals will give up their lives for something they sincerely believe is true. Radical Islam has encouraged martyrdom. Cult leaders have led hundreds of followers at a time to suicide. Even the Jewish Zealots of Jesus' day sometimes sacrificed themselves on behalf of their beliefs. However, as Strobel also notes, people won't die for their religious beliefs *if they know their beliefs are false.*

The original followers of Jesus would have known the difference, as all but one of the original apostles died for their faith. As author J.P. Moreland shared in an interview:

> The apostles were willing to die for something they had seen with their own eyes and touched with their own hands. They were in a unique position not to just believe Jesus rose from the dead but to know for sure. And when you've got eleven credible people with no ulterior motives, with nothing to gain and a lot to lose, who all agree they observed something with their own eyes—now you've got some difficulty explaining that away.[3]

As we continue our conversation in this chapter, we'll take a closer look at the earliest followers of Jesus and the growth of early Christianity. As even the 2006 CNN special *After Jesus: the First Christians* observed, one of the most fascinating aspects of Christianity was its rapid growth throughout the Roman Empire.[4]

## The Explosion of Christianity

Throughout this book, I (John) have shared from an interview with Dr. William Lane Craig in a response to an ABC special *The Search for Jesus*. We've already looked at four key facts historians must face about Jesus. Now we're ready to look at the next one: "The fifth fundamental fact that any credible historical hypothesis concerning the fate of Jesus of Nazareth has to explain is the very origin of the disciples' belief that God had raised Jesus of Nazareth from the dead.

"You see, it's an indisputable fact that Christianity sprang into being in the middle of the first century. Now, why did this movement arise? Where did it come from?"[5]

N.T. Wright provided a colorful explanation of this growth during my interview with him at his home office in England. He shared that "the origin of Christianity is actually itself one of the most extraordinary phenomenon in the history of the world. In A.D. 20 there's no such thing as a Christian church. By A.D. 120, the emperor in Rome is getting letters of worry from one of his proconsuls in northern Turkey about what to do about these Christians. So in that century, you have this extraordinary thing suddenly appearing out of nowhere. All the early Christians for whom we have actual evidence would say, 'I'll tell you why it's happened. It's because of Jesus of Nazareth and the fact that He was raised from the dead.'"[6]

---

"It was not only friendly eyewitnesses that the early preachers had to reckon with; there were others less well disposed who were also conversant with the main facts of the ministry and death of Jesus. The disciples could not afford to risk inaccuracies (not to speak of willful manipulation of the facts), which would at once be exposed by those who would be only too glad to do so."

—**F.F. BRUCE,** *THE NEW TESTAMENT DOCUMENTS: ARE THEY RELIABLE?*[7]

---

## The Basis of Belief

Dr. Craig's research has shown that "all scholars agree that the reason for the birth of this Christian movement in Palestine in the middle of the first century is because these first disciples suddenly and sincerely came to believe that the God of Israel had raised Jesus of Nazareth from the dead. But now that brings forth an even deeper question: Where in the world did they come up with that outlandish belief?"

Dr. Ben Witherington responds by noting, "I would say that in the first century A.D. it took a great deal of courage to be a Christian and to claim that a crucified manual worker named Jesus from Nazareth, against all expectations, turned out to be the savior of the world.

"Now this is a fantastic claim. Early Jews were not looking for a crucified Messiah, so far as we can see. Greco-Roman people were certainly not looking for a crucified manual worker being their Messiah. So here we have these people evangelizing the world and claiming this is the truth that you need to know about—that Jesus died and rose again—and this demonstrates who he is. It takes an awful lot of guts to put that message out there."

## The Jewish Perspective

This rapid growth of Christianity appears even more spectacular when we consider the first-century Jewish worldview. Craig explained that "to appreciate how outlandish their new belief in Jesus was, you must understand something about the disciples' Jewish background. They had placed their faith in Jesus of Nazareth as the promised Jewish Messiah who would deliver Israel from her enemies. Yet, there is no conception in antecedent Judaism of a Messiah who, instead of coming and conquering Israel's enemies, would be vanquished and executed by them and executed in so shameful and disgraceful a manner as crucifixion. This was simply unheard of in Jewish messianic expectations.

"Moreover, the idea that the Messiah would then be raised from the dead is simply unknown in Judaism. Couple with this the fact that, according to Old Testament law, anyone executed by hanging on a tree is thereby shown to be accursed by God, and the Jews applied this fact to death by crucifixion as well. Now, what this meant is that the crucifixion showed Jesus of Nazareth out to be a man literally under the curse of God. It wasn't just that now their beloved master was dead and they had lost their rabbi. It was worse than that. For three years they had been following a man accursed by God, a heretic. So the crucifixion put a question mark on everything that these men had believed in and entrusted about Jesus.

"In addition to that, Judaism had no concept of a resurrection occurring within human history. Read the Jewish literature prior to and up through the first century. You will find nothing parallel to the resurrection of Jesus in Jewish thought. In Jewish thinking, the resurrection always occurred *after* the end of the world. It was always a general resurrection of *all* the righteous dead. There was no conception of the resurrection of an isolated individual apart from the general resurrection, in advance, within history, to glory and immortality. That's why, as a historian, I must conclude that these disciples really did see the resurrected Jesus, and this changed their lives and the way they thought."

## We Saw Him!

*"Now you can say a lot about what people are willing to live for, but what people are actually willing to die for is another question. These early Christians were prepared to die for an honest testimony about having seen the risen Jesus."*

—DR. BEN WITHERINGTON[8]

Dr. Habermas emphasizes in his writings the bridge between what the disciples think they saw and what they did see. According to him, "I imagine a lot of people are saying, 'I'll grant you that the disciples *believed* they saw Jesus.' How do you get from *thought* they saw to they *saw?*

"The fact that they *thought* they saw the risen Jesus is important for two reasons. Those five facts I evidenced before [see pages 84-86], those facts tell me, number one, naturalistic theories don't work. The disciples *believed* they saw the risen Jesus. Some people say they saw hallucinations. But using only those historical facts, we can show hallucinations don't work. All the naturalistic theories fail.

"Then, there is a second reason their *belief* that they saw Jesus turns into they actually *saw* Jesus. It is because these same facts that everybody admits include a lot of good evidences that they *really* saw him. Their lives were changed. It was a central proclamation. Otherwise, how do you get the intellectual skeptic Paul on board? How do you get Jesus' own unbelieving brother James on board? How do you get Thomas on board? Every one of them agreed *it was something they saw.*

"What does Christianity have that other religions don't have? Jim Jones's followers believed he was the Messiah. They were wrong. So were the followers of David Koresh. The Comet Hale-Bopp people believed a UFO was coming for them. Anybody can be wrong about beliefs. People can even die for false beliefs.

"But what was different about the disciples was they didn't just say Jesus was the Messiah and he was raised from the dead. Their central claim was 'We *saw* him.' At the same time that Paul mentions the many postresurrection appearances of Jesus in 1 Corinthians 15, he says, 'If Christ has not been raised from the dead, then our faith is in vain.'"

Let me (John) illustrate. I would venture it is safe to say that funerals have convinced you that resurrections *don't* happen. What would it take to persuade you that a friend had come back from the dead?

Let's say your best friend is a lawyer, and he is respected and credible in everything he does. One afternoon he tells you, "I'm going to meet my mother for lunch." You believe him. The next week, his mother dies of a heart attack. You go to her funeral and watch as she is buried. A month later your friend tells you, "I want you to know that I saw my mother last night." This time you *don't* believe him.

Before, you believed your friend. But then you *didn't* believe him. Why? Because you've never seen someone come back from the dead. Philosopher David Hume said it would be a miracle if a dead man came back to life because "that has never been observed in any age or country. There must, therefore, be a uniform experience against every miraculous event, otherwise that event would not merit that appellation."[9]

Hume is right. But as C.S. Lewis has said, if a miracle has never happened before, then of course it has never happened before. The only way that we can know a miracle has occurred is to investigate the historical evidence.

So, because of your past experience that dead people stay dead, you don't believe your friend's declaration that he saw his mother after she died. Maybe he just mistook someone else for his mom. Maybe he was hallucinating. Maybe in his grief he just wanted to believe she was still around and had a vision of her. But he keeps insisting, "No! I really *saw* my mother."

The next day you go to the store to do some shopping. As you are walking through one of the aisles, your friend's mother comes up to you and says hello. She starts talking to you about old times—things only you two know and remember. On her left arm you can see she has the same scar you remember she got while cooking lunch. It's the same body!

As she walks away, you're bewildered. How can she be alive? You saw her, and you shook hands with her. But you're still having a hard time believing it. You can relate to those in the Gospel account of whom it says, "When they saw him, they worshiped him; *but some doubted.*"[10] As you continue your way through the aisle, you meet 12 friends who are also shopping at the same store. You wonder if you ought to tell them that your friend—and now you—have actually seen his mother. But just at that moment, she shows up again, and all 13 of you see her.

Now the evidence is starting to mount up in your mind and you are convinced she is alive. Somehow, some way, she is alive. You all saw her. Later that night at your church, 500 people are gathered for a church service. Your friend's mother comes through the side door and walks up to the platform and speaks to the whole congregation. Now you are a part of a group of 500 people who have all seen and heard her at the same time.

The disciples didn't just say, "We *believe* we saw Jesus." They said, "We *saw* Jesus." Somehow, we have to do justice to their point. Yes, the disciples believed. They believed Jesus was raised. They believed Jesus was the Messiah. But besides that, they have evidence here that nobody else has: "I saw you at the same store," and "We saw you in a group." If my faith is based on seeing you at a store, and on seeing you along with 500 other people, I think it's pretty firm. That's one reason the disciples were so excited and so convinced. *Seeing is believing.*

## What *Is* the Big Deal About Jesus?

As we wrapped up our interview time together, I asked Dr. Craig to summarize what we had discussed. He reiterated, "With respect to historical hypotheses concerning the fate of Jesus of Nazareth, there are four fundamental facts agreed upon by the majority of New Testament scholars who have studied this and written on the subject that must be explained (in addition to his death):

- *Number one:* The honorable burial of Jesus of Nazareth by Joseph of Arimathea in a tomb.

- *Number two:* The discovery of Jesus' empty tomb by a group of his women followers early on Sunday morning following his crucifixion.

- *Number three:* The experience of various individuals and groups of people at various locations and under various circumstances of postmortem appearances of Jesus alive from the dead.

- *Number four:* The very origin of the Christian faith itself in the disciples coming suddenly and sincerely to believe that God had raised Jesus of Nazareth from the dead.

"Those are the facts that need to be explained. What is the best explanation for these? I believe that when you assess the various alternatives, the various live options, using the ordinary canons of historical assessments—such as explanatory power, explanatory scope, the degree of contrivance, plausibility, the degree to which it is in accord with accepted beliefs, the degree to which the hypothesis outstrips rival hypotheses—that the best explanation for these facts is that God raised Jesus of Nazareth from the dead."

Dr. Habermas ended his interview with similar conclusions. "We have framed this argument to facts that believers *and* unbelievers hold in common. We've started with twelve. There are really more than that, but we reduced it down to five. What we want the critic to understand here is that these are your facts. They're in *your* books. They're in everyone's books. What do you do with these five facts?

"The disciples *believed* they had seen the risen Jesus. How do you stop this path from *thought they saw* to *really saw?* You come up with a naturalistic theory. Then, I want them to take one of those and run with it. Don't hide behind, 'Well, granted, *something* happened.' No. You've given us enough facts here to say the earliest eyewitnesses believed they saw the risen Jesus. We need an alternative if the answer is not going to be they *really* saw Him.

"But strangely enough, most scholars won't take that route, either in their books or in dialogues. They feel like they're trapped. They will say, 'If I take this theory, you're going to come after me.'

"I'll say, 'Now, wait a minute. I'm using your facts. If you don't believe the conclusion, what's this missing X? What do you think really happened?'

"They usually at that point will opt out of the discussion any way they can. But if they *do* take a naturalistic theory, my assertion is, *the known historical facts,* those admitted by all scholars, are sufficient to refute those naturalistic theories as well as give the best evidences for the resurrection. If you're going to grant as much as they grant, let's follow this thing to a conclusion. You have given me five facts. *Explain* the five facts. Don't hide behind, 'Something happened.' Tell me what these facts indicate. I think we're pushing straight toward the resurrection of Christ."

### What If He Did?

When I (John) asked Darrell Bock, "If God did raise Jesus from the dead, what was he trying to tell us?" Darrell said, "I think the gospel is the good news that God has provided a way to come into your life forever, not as a ticket, but into a relationship. He has provided the way to that relationship through the person and work of Jesus Christ, not only the sacrifice for sins, but the provision of his very own Spirit coming into your life so that you can relate to God on a healthy level and overcome the sinfulness that is inherent in you.

"The good news is that God is committed to that relationship—so committed that he sent his only Son to die that it might take place.

The only requirement that exists—it's a serious requirement—is that you believe that he's done that for you and, in faith, you ask for that relationship through Jesus Christ. It's that simple, and that demanding, because once God comes into your life, he's in it to do a marvelous work, a work that grounds you in a relationship with God that will never end."[11]

Conclusion:

# What Should I Do with Jesus?

If you've stayed with us all the way to this point in our journey together, you are likely someone passionately seeking truth, someone who desires to know what the big deal is about Jesus. Perhaps what you've learned has increased your understanding and concern to the point you realize you have an important choice to make. If Jesus is who he said he was, how should you respond?

Three of our experts in this book had these words to say in that regard;

- *Dr. Craig Evans:* "If a person is going to say Jesus is not going to be important in my life, I'm not going to believe in him, then they're going to have to say that for other reasons besides historical....the evidence is there, the sources are there, the picture is clear and coherent, and in my academic opinion, the picture is quite compelling."

- *Dr. N.T. Wright:* "Therefore, the historian, whether that historian be a secularist, a Muslim, a Christian, whatever—the historian has to ask, 'How do we explain the fact this movement spread like wildfire with Jesus as the Messiah, even though Jesus had been crucified?' The answer has to be, 'It can only be because he was raised from the dead.'"

- *Dr. William Lane Craig:* "The claim of the resurrection of Jesus alone makes him unique among the religious figures of the world. The fact that we have good evidence for it makes it more than unique. It makes it astonishing."[1]

Our choice must be more than religion. It must involve a relationship. The process of choosing to follow Jesus involves some significant acknowledgments.

First, our relationship with God is broken, and we don't know how to fix it. We may believe God exists, but he feels a million miles away and we don't know why. The problem was well stated by the Jewish prophet Isaiah, who confessed generations ago, "All of us, like sheep, have strayed away. We have left God's paths to follow our own."[2]

Ever lied? Ever had an impure thought? Ever shouted an unkind word? We all have. God calls these unkind and hurtful actions sin. Our first step toward following Jesus is to acknowledge there is a God, and it's not us. We are the ones in need of a higher power, not a power within ourselves.

According to scripture, our wrongful thoughts and actions hold severe consequences. Isaiah penned the words, "It's your sins that have cut you off from God."[3] Another Bible writer explained, "The person who sins is the one who will die."[4] To be candid about it, Jesus said our sins, no matter how great or small, will result in eternal punishment in hell.[5] We don't like to talk about it, but that's the bad news in this story. We can ignore the information or change the end of the story.

The good news in this narrative is that the price to change our situation has already been paid. The cost? The cross. According to the prophets and apostles...

- "The LORD laid on him the sins of us all."[6]

- "He was pierced for our rebellion, crushed for our sins. He was beaten so we could be whole. He was whipped so we could be healed."[7]

- "He bore the sins of many and interceded for rebels."[8]
- "Christ suffered for our sins once for all time. He never sinned, but he died for sinners to bring you safely home to God."[9]

Jesus said the primary reason he came into our world was to rescue us from divine judgment and provide a way for us to enjoy a close, personal relationship with him. He promised us we could have our wrongs fully and freely forgiven, our guilt removed, and our joy restored.

To enjoy these benefits, we are called to accept the challenge to ask for forgiveness from our wrongs (an act of humility) and trust in Jesus as God's only answer to our situation. How can we know this? From the most primitive times, the writers of God have communicated:

> Seek the LORD while you can find him. Call on him now while he is near. Let the wicked change their ways and banish the very thought of doing wrong. Let them turn to the LORD that he may have mercy on them. Yes, turn to our God, for he will forgive generously.[10]

Jesus personally promised, "I tell you the truth, those who listen to my message and believe in God who sent me have eternal life. They will never be condemned for their sins, but they have already passed from death into life."[11] In a prayer to his Father the night before his crucifixion, Jesus shared, "This is the way to have eternal life—to know you, the only true God, and Jesus Christ, the one you sent to earth."[12]

The best part about this deal is that it's not based on the quality of our performance. Jesus certainly wants us to do what is right, but following him is based on his gift of grace. Our part is to take the step of faith to open this life-changing gift.

Paul, the great missionary and apostle, described this mystery, writing to early Christ-followers that "God saved you by his grace when you believed. And you can't take credit for this; it is a gift from

God. Salvation is not a reward for the good things we have done, so none of us can boast about it."[13]

The big deal about Jesus is ultimately his great love for us. He has done all of the work already. He invites us to embrace him in an intimate relationship for all eternity. Are you ready to join this spiritual revolution? Will you choose the way of Jesus?

There is no magic prayer to start the journey, but we'd like to offer a model to guide you. If you don't know where to begin, start with:

> *God, I ask your son Jesus to enter my life as my leader and rescuer. I know I've messed up. I've sinned. Please forgive me. I believe Jesus came back to life from the dead and place my faith in him for eternal life. I choose to follow Jesus from this moment forward. Please show me how to live for you.*

If you just made this request of Jesus, congratulations! Your life will never be the same. You will experience forgiveness, love, joy, and a peace through life's ups and downs. If you're coming back to begin afresh with Jesus, we want to encourage you in your spiritual journey as well. No matter where you've been, Jesus wants to help you move forward on an adventure of faith in close relationship with him. He promises to enter your life to give you a new purpose and passion.

We also invite you to let us know about any decision you have made or new growth you have experienced. Please e-mail us at staff@johnankerberg.org with your story. We'll be thrilled to share additional spiritual growth resources in return. Allow us the privilege of enjoying together your new response to make Jesus a big deal in your life.

# Alternative Ideas on What Happened to Jesus' Body [1]

Ever since the time of Jesus, people have attempted to offer alternative theories to explain his bodily resurrection. Historically, many theories have been proposed, but none has yet met with general acceptance, even among critics. The following list is representative of the ideas that have surfaced over the years:

*The swoon theory* claims that Jesus never died on the cross but only passed out (or "swooned"). After his crucifixion (which included a spear thrust into his heart), he was taken down from the cross, wrapped in 75 pounds of linen and spices, and placed in a tomb. Yet somehow he revived. Of course, this theory also requires that Jesus died at some later point in time.

Professor Gary Habermas notes:

> It is self-contradictory. What you have from the "swoon" is a living Jesus but not a resurrected Jesus, and here's how it works. Jesus should have died on the cross; he didn't. He should have died in the tomb; he didn't. He certainly can't roll the stone away. No problem. He did. Now, Strauss didn't believe in a guard, but for those who

believe a guard is sitting out there, he works his way through the guards. But here's the problem for Strauss. Again, you have: he didn't die on the cross; didn't die in the tomb; couldn't roll the stone. He comes to where the disciples are. *[Knock, knock, knock]* He knocks on the door. What's this man going to look like? He's a human Jesus. He's been crucified. He's worked the wounds open again. He's bleeding from the scalp. His hair has not even been washed. I mean, you've got sweat and blood, and he's worked the side open again. And he's hunched over, he's limping, he's pale. And *[knock, knock, knock]:* "I told you I would rise again from the dead." One problem, Strauss said, with the swoon theory is, you get a Jesus who is alive, but you don't get a Jesus who is *raised.* Now, Strauss does not believe in the resurrection, but he knows the disciples did. And the "swoon" doesn't get you from A to B. You get this kind of Jesus: "Lord, come on in. Get a chair. Get a pail of water. Call the doctor."

To paraphrase Strauss, the disciples would have gotten a doctor before they proclaimed him risen because here's Peter over in the corner saying, "Oh, boy! Someday I'm going to have a resurrection body just like his." And that, by the way, is the proclamation that is most tied to the resurrection of Jesus: that believers will be raised. Now, again, Strauss doesn't think believers are going to be raised and he doesn't think there's a guard and he doesn't think that Jesus was raised, but if you can't get that belief on the disciples' part, it doesn't work. And the problem is, "swoon" can't account for the experiences that the disciples had that they thought were appearances of the risen Jesus.[2]

*The Passover Plot theory* is a version of the swoon theory. This idea suggests that Jesus intentionally planned to fake his death to give the appearance he rose from the dead. He conspired with

Judas to betray him to the Jewish authorities and with Joseph of Arimathea to see to it that he was given a strong potion on the cross which would put him into a deathlike trance. Appearing dead to the Roman authorities, he was to be taken off the cross and laid in a tomb—where he would revive after a short time and then reappear as resurrected to his followers.

But the unexpected spear thrust led to his unforeseen death. Joseph had him buried in an unknown tomb. His followers came upon the intended original place of burial, found the prearranged grave clothes, and falsely concluded from this that Jesus was alive.

*The stolen body theory* suggests that Jesus' followers stole or moved his body to make it appear he had been resurrected. This would, of course, make his followers frauds. Other versions of this theory claim that the Jews, Romans, or Joseph of Arimathea moved the body.

Dr. William Lane Craig notes,

> The empty tomb story enjoys multiple independent lines of evidence. For example, the burial account supports the empty tomb story. If the burial account of Jesus is historically accurate, then the inference that the tomb was found empty is not very far at hand because the resurrection faith could not have arisen and flourished in the face of a closed tomb.[3]

*The hallucination theory* argues that all the people who had claimed to see the resurrected Jesus (yes, including the 500-plus who saw him at one time!) were only seeing visions or were hallucinating. This theory severely struggles with the physical acts Jesus displayed after his resurrection, such as eating a fish or his disciples physically touching his hands and side.

*The telegraph theory* believes that the spiritually ascended Jesus telegraphed images of himself from heaven to the minds of his followers on earth. These images were so graphic that they all mistakenly thought they had physically seen Jesus alive. The major problem here is the question of the empty tomb. In reality, this theory must be combined with another theory that covers the empty tomb rather than as a stand-alone idea.

*The mistaken identity theory* advocates that the 11 disciples misidentified a complete stranger as Jesus. But wouldn't a close friend at the very least recognize his voice during a conversation?

*The séance theory* suggests that Jesus was raised in the same way a spirit is manifested in a séance. Though the practice was not even permissible among Jews, this claim would be required to prove that such a habit was in use by at least hundreds of Jews during this period of first-century Judaism—something historians do not suggest in their studies.

*The annihilation theory* simply argues that Jesus' body unexplainably disintegrated in some unknown way.

### The Making of a Legend

"The time span necessary for significant accrual of legend concerning the events of the gospels would place us in the second century A.D., just the time in fact when the legendary apocryphal gospels were born. These are the legendary accounts sought by the critics."

—DR. WILLIAM LANE CRAIG[4]

*The resurrection as legend theory* teaches that Jesus never physically existed in history. Some go so far as to reason that the disciples simply borrowed the idea of a resurrected deity from the pagan religions of their day.

### They Don't Even Believe Themselves

"Critical scholars have generally rejected naturalistic theories as a whole, judging that they are incapable of explaining known data....That even such critical scholars have rejected these naturalistic theories is a significant epitaph for the failure of these views."

—DR. GARY HABERMAS, *ANCIENT EVIDENCE FOR THE LIFE OF JESUS*[5]

## What Did the Disciples See?

When the disciples saw the resurrected Jesus, what did they see?

1. nothing

2. hallucinations

3. a ghost

4. a vision/dream (mental only)

5. a different person

6. Jesus, who was still alive

7. Jesus alive again from the dead

Numbers one through five are impossible. There were too many people in too many places to see nothing, some spiritual vision, or a different person. This could also have been easily disproved by early opponents of Christianity. This leaves us with the option that Jesus was still alive, meaning he either survived a crucifixion or he really *did* come back to life. Because we have several confirming signs that Jesus physically died (see chapter 9), then the most likely choice is that Jesus really came back to life. As Christians proclaimed from that time forward, he is risen!

| Major Issues of the Alternative Theories to Explain the Empty Tomb | |
| --- | --- |
| **ALTERNATE THEORY** | **THEORY'S WEAKNESSES** |
| Swoon theory | Powerful evidence for death and burial of Jesus |
| Passover Plot theory | Resurrection appearances; inconsistent with Jewish prophecies regarding the Messiah |
| Stolen body theory | Difficult logistics of operation; consistent beliefs lived out by his followers even under persecution |
| Hallucination theory | Numbers of people involved |

| | |
|---|---|
| Telegraph theory | Doesn't explain empty tomb or the physical acts of Jesus (eating, talking, disciples touching wounds) |
| Mistaken identity theory | Close friends would have recognized the difference |
| Wrong tomb theory | Publicity surrounding Jesus' death; eyewitnesses of burial |
| Séance theory | Not generally practiced within Jewish culture; numbers of people required to be involved |
| Annihilation theory | Resurrection appearances; explanation of how theory occurred |
| Resurrection as legend theory | Resurrection appearances; lives of disciples; influence on centuries of history |

**Appendix B:**

# Alleged Contradictions in the Crucifixion and Resurrection Accounts in the Gospels

### By Dr. John Ankerberg

Quick or careless readings of the four Gospels—which present the details of Jesus' death, burial, and resurrection—have led some people to assume that the accounts contradict each other; therefore, the resurrection itself is questionable or cannot be believed. So we must ask: Do the four resurrection narratives of the Gospels of Matthew, Mark, Luke, and John in any way contradict each other?

We must start by remembering that the Gospel writers are independently reporting these events. A hallmark of independent reporting is differences in content. In a court of law, for example, it is *always true* that four witnesses describing a traffic accident (or a crime, or any other incident) will each supply different information. Each witness notices and reports those things that are unique, relevant, or important to them. The same is true for the Gospel writers. Each one devotes differing amounts of space and detail to the events. Each mentions some details that the others do not.

If every Gospel writer recorded the events in precisely the same way, giving precisely the same details, this would be evidence of collusion, not independent testimony. There is no reason to demand that the Gospel writers should have reported the same exact details. When critics charge that contradictions exist merely because the accounts differ, they are being unfair. They are holding the Gospel authors to a standard to which they would not subject themselves.

For example, when the *Challenger* space shuttle exploded or the World Trade Center was attacked on 9/11, many of us probably flipped from channel to channel to catch different news accounts of the events that were taking place. Different facts were noted or omitted by different reporters. But these differences didn't lead us to conclude that the incidents never happened.

Furthermore, if one of the channels added new information or gave a slightly different emphasis in their report, did we assume that the various news accounts could not be harmonized? Not at all. The same is true for the Gospels. When one writer gives additional information or places his own emphasis on one part of the story, and reasonable attempts at harmonization successfully blend the elements together, no contradiction need be assumed.

Let's look now at some of the alleged contradictions in the Gospel accounts, and see whether they can be harmonized.

## 1. Who carried Jesus' cross—Jesus himself, or Simon of Cyrene?

The synoptic Gospels (Matthew, Mark, and Luke) report the following: "As they led [Jesus] away, they seized Simon from Cyrene, who was on his way in from the country, and put the cross on him and made him carry it behind Jesus" (Luke 23:26, also Matthew 27:32; Mark 15:21). But John seems to suggest that Jesus carried it the whole way himself: "Carrying his own cross, he went out to the place of the Skull (which in Aramaic is called Golgotha)" (John 19:17).

Because of the beatings and other sufferings Jesus endured following his trials, Jesus was in all probability now extremely weak. A reasonable solution to this apparent contradiction is that Jesus was able to carry the cross only part of the way (John); Simon the Cyrene then carried it the remainder of the way (Matthew, Mark, Luke). It is also possible that Jesus carried part of the cross all of the way while Simon carried the other piece.

## 2. Did Jesus drink the wine mixture given to him on the cross or refuse it?

- Matthew says Jesus tasted the mixture but refused to drink it (27:34).

- Mark says he was offered the wine but did not take it (15:23).

- Luke mentions only that he was offered wine vinegar (23:36).

- John says that Jesus "received the drink," implying he drank it (19:29-30).

Furthermore, Matthew says the wine was mixed with gall; Mark says it was mixed with myrrh; and Luke and John say it was mixed with vinegar.

We should remember that Jesus was alive on the cross for some six hours. The crucifixion accounts make it clear that on three *separate* occasions a wine mixture was offered to him.

The first offer, as recorded in Matthew and Mark, was made by the soldiers *before* Jesus was crucified. This drink contained wine mixed with gall or myrrh. Customarily this was offered to condemned prisoners as a mild analgesic just prior to crucifixion to lessen the pain. But Jesus *refused* that drink (Matthew 27:34; Mark 15:23).

Luke records a second offer by the soldiers to Jesus *after* he was crucified (23:36), this time of wine vinegar or sour wine, a common drink. No mention, however, is made of whether Jesus accepted it.

The third offer, in this instance of wine vinegar, was made to Jesus *shortly before* his death. It occurred after he had uttered the phrase, "My God, my God, why have you forsaken me?" (Matthew 27:46).

Matthew, Mark, and John mention it, and all three agree that Jesus *accepted the drink* (John 19:28-30; Matthew 27:48; Mark 15:36). A careful reading of the text reveals no contradiction.

## 3. What was written on the inscription placed above Jesus on the cross?

- Matthew wrote, "This is Jesus, the king of the Jews" (27:37).
- Mark wrote, "The king of the Jews" (15:25).
- Luke wrote, "This is the king of the Jews" (23:38).
- John wrote, "Jesus of Nazareth, the king of the Jews" (19:19).

All four writers mention that the sign included "The king of the Jews," with Matthew adding "This is Jesus" and John adding "Jesus of Nazareth." In its entirety, the sign probably read "This is Jesus of Nazareth, the king of the Jews." The gospel writers' piecemeal citations of the sign, however, presents no contradiction. Each author cites it as best suits his purpose. To do this is not to mislead.

## 4. Did both thieves insult Jesus, or only one?

Matthew and Mark mention that both thieves insulted Jesus (Matthew 27:44; Mark 15:32), whereas Luke has only one insulting him (23:39-40). John does not mention the incident.

In resolving this apparent contradiction, we again need to remember that Jesus was alive on the cross for about six hours. It is perfectly reasonable to think both criminals initially insulted Jesus, but as the time passed, one of them, after observing Jesus and listening to him, changed his mind and later rebuked the other criminal for his insults.

## 5. What were Jesus' last words on the cross?

If one does not read the texts carefully, it would appear that

Matthew and Mark assert that Jesus' last cry was, "My God, my God, why have you forsaken me?" (Matthew 27:46; Mark 15:34). But shortly after this statement, both authors also record that Jesus "cried out again in a loud voice" and then breathed his last ("gave up his spirit") (Matthew 27:50; Mark 15:37).

In other words, both Matthew and Mark refer to a yet later saying of Jesus although they do not identify the words spoken. Luke identifies this loud cry as, "Father, into your hands I commit my spirit" (23:46). John informs us that Jesus uttered, "It is finished" (19:30), though he does not say that Jesus spoke this in a loud voice; thus it presumably immediately preceded Jesus' last words as mentioned by Luke.

What this means is that after Jesus had cried out, "My God, my God, why have you forsaken me?" a brief period of time elapsed. Then, during the last minutes of his life, he uttered, "It is finished," and immediately after that, loudly cried, "Father, into your hands I commit my spirit." At this point, he died. This is not the only possible reconstruction, but it perfectly harmonizes the Gospel evidence. One author adds a saying another leaves out, but this is only to be expected from independent reporting as opposed to collusion.

## 6. How many women visited Jesus' tomb?

Do the four resurrection narratives contradict each other concerning the number of women who went to Jesus' tomb?

- Matthew mentions *two* women—Mary Magdalene and the other Mary (28:1).

- Mark mentions *three* women—Mary Magdalene, Mary the mother of James, and Salome (16:1).

- Luke *does not specify a number* but simply mentions "the women" (24:1).

- John mentions *one* woman, Mary Magdalene (20:1).

Again, we must keep in mind that writers have every right to select certain facts according to their literary purposes. To do this does not necessarily misrepresent the historical evidence. We cannot know all the reasons why one author selects information that another does not. It would make a writer's job virtually impossible if he or she had to list all the reasons for including certain details and omitting others.

Mark feels it is important, for some reason, to report that Salome was at the tomb, while Matthew does not. Perhaps Salome was the woman, or one of several women, who recounted the events to Mark. Perhaps Matthew does not mention Salome because he documented the event from a source that did not include her.

Some critics charge that Luke disagrees with Matthew and Mark because he mentions only "the women." But this argument is without force. None of the gospel writers say it was *only* two women, or *only* one woman, or *only* three women. Each writer mentions those he wants to recognize perhaps according to special literary emphases or because this is all the information he presently knows or can readily substantiate. *But none of them give contradictory information.* If one of the four writers had said *only* so-and-so went to the tomb, and another had said *only* somebody else went, then we would have a contradiction.

In referring merely to "the women," Luke does not contradict Matthew and Mark; he merely is less specific. However, does John contradict the other three writers because he records only one woman, Mary Magdalene, going to the tomb? Two perfectly reasonable explanations present themselves here.

First, all the women may have set out for the tomb, with Mary arriving first. John simply records the earliest arrival. Or second, John may have chosen to write only about Mary, even though he could have written about all the women. These possibilities are, of course, not mutually exclusive.

As with the other writers, John does not say that *only* Mary Magdalene went to the tomb. But he is perfectly free to concentrate on Mary Magdalene, especially if her experience is important to his writing interests. He probably features her for a number of reasons:

1) After the resurrection, Jesus appeared to her first (and not to one of the disciples); 2) Mary looked into the tomb and saw the two angels (John 20:11-12); 3) Mary personally met the resurrected Jesus near the empty tomb (verses 11-18); and 4) Jesus commissioned her to go and tell the disciples the good news (verse 17).

The disciples who heard the women tell their stories may have heard bits of information from each of the women, most of it from just one, or most of it from several.

In *The Easter Enigma,* John Wenham suggests that "Luke's is a straightforward account written from Joanna's point of view (Luke 8:3; 24:10), whereas Mark's is an account written from the point of view of the other three women."[1] Similarly, John may have written his version strictly from Mary Magdalene's viewpoint, assuming that the majority of Christians had already known that this group of women went to the tomb. Perhaps he decided to share additional details of what had happened to Mary Magdalene because people were not as aware of it.

Indeed, when Luke mentions "the others with them" (24:10), we could even assume that more than three women were present at the tomb on Easter morning. If Luke is describing the women who actually visited the tomb, then there were at least five. Joanna and "the others" signifies at least one more person than Salome. It is also possible that the "other women" to whom Luke alludes were part of the group who reported to the disciples.

To sum up, we know that at least three women visited the tomb, and possibly more. The resurrection accounts are not contradictory. None of the writers state that only a set number of women visited the tomb. Rather, each selected details from a broader pool of evidence according to his purpose in writing.

## 7. How many angels were at the tomb?

An apparent difficulty of the resurrection narratives is that Matthew and Mark refer to *one* angel (Matthew 28:2-4; Mark 16:5), while Luke and John refer to *two* (Luke 24:5; John 20:12).

Here the principle we emphasized in the last question again applies. Although the four Gospel writers deal with the same event, they are not obligated to include every detail known to them or, for that matter, the same details the others record in their accounts.

Mark merely recounts that the women encounter an angel sitting on the right side of the tomb, who proceeds to give them a message (he compresses the story here as Matthew has done at other places in his resurrection account). Luke, on the other hand, supplies more details. He states that, in addition to the angel who speaks, a second angel is present. Apparently the second angel remains silent.

> It should be said once and for all that the mention by one evangelist of two angels and by another of one does not constitute a contradiction or discrepancy. If there were two, there was one....Contradiction would only be created if the writer who mentioned the one should go on to say explicitly that there was only one....It needs to be remembered that we are dealing with two *descriptions of* an event, and not with two witnesses replying to cross-examination.... These witnesses are not answering the question "How many?"—they are giving (as all descriptions must be) incomplete descriptions of a complex event.[2]

In fact, at Jesus' resurrection, *many* different angels may have been intermittently present at the tomb. Although Matthew, Mark, Luke, and John differ on details concerning the number of angels, their accounts do not contradict. Rather, they are complementary.

## 8. Were these beings men or angels?

- Matthew reports "an angel" (28:2).
- Mark describes "a young man" (16:5).
- Luke writes "two men" (24:4).
- John reports "two angels" (20:12).

Do these accounts conflict, or were the Gospel writers confused on this point? Whenever angels appear to people in scripture, they are almost always said to take the form of men. This is not surprising; it may be deliberate on their part to reduce the anxiety of those with whom they come into contact. But they often eventually reveal their angelic identity in some unique way, as in Matthew 28:2-3; at times they may keep it entirely hidden, as is plain from Hebrews 13:2. Therefore, it is not contradictory for the four Gospel writers to refer to the angels as men or as angels. Both are correct.

Regardless, Matthew and John are specific: Matthew writes, "an angel of the Lord"; John, "two angels in white." Although Luke and Mark describe their appearance as men, Luke clearly identifies them as angels, noting they were "in clothes that gleamed like lightning" (24:4). Even though the Bible frequently describes angels as men, little doubt usually remains as to their angelic identity. In fact, at times angels are first described as men and later as angels in the very same passage (for example, in Judges 13:2-22). This biblical phenomenon, in all probability, properly explains how Luke and Mark understood the identity of the "men" who appeared to the women at the tomb; and it underscores how important it is to read the resurrection narratives in light of these other parts of scripture.

## 9. Who visited the tomb first?

As we have already noted, John may have concentrated on documenting Mary Magdalene's visit to the tomb either: 1) to the exclusion of the other women, or 2) because she was probably the first person to arrive at the tomb. The second option is preferable. It is quite possible that all the women had planned to meet at the tomb and left their homes at approximately the same time. Mary arrived first, observed the empty tomb, and before her companions arrived, ran to tell Peter and John about it. Thus, Matthew, Mark, and Luke could talk generally about all the women going to the tomb and they would be correct; John could report specifically that Mary reached the tomb first and he would be correct.

This reconstruction of the event would explain John's account as it stands. The other Gospel accounts would also permit it, especially Mark and Matthew, which at this juncture have unannounced breaks in their resurrection narratives. These occur between Mark 16:1 and 16:2 and between Matthew 28:1 and 28:2 and again between verses 4 and 5. These breaks allow for the possibility that Mary came first to the tomb and that the other women arrived shortly after she left. Furthermore, Luke's inclusion of Mary with the other women who report to the disciples what happened at the tomb (Luke 24:9-11) does not conflict with this.

But there is at least one more plausible reconstruction as well: Mary arrived at the tomb first while it was still dark and was still there when the other women arrived. In essence, all the women mentioned by the Gospel writers, as a group, arrived at the tomb at about the same time. Whichever of these reconstructions one prefers, neither of them poses contradictions for the resurrection accounts.

## 10. Did they visit the tomb when it was dark or light?

The specific *time* the women went to the tomb has also been called into question. Matthew says "at dawn" (Matthew 28:1), while Mark has "just after sunrise" (Mark 16:2). But here, too, the objection is flimsy.

An announcement of an Easter "sunrise" service nicely illustrates this. One reporter might state that the service is "at dawn," while another says "just after sunrise." As we know, "at dawn" includes "just after sunrise." If today's writers frequently do not use precise language concerning time, why should we expect it of the Gospel authors? Both phrases, "at dawn" and "just after sunrise," can involve a significant span of time. If we say we went to the beach at dawn, the hearer understands that we could mean anything from some minutes before sunrise to some minutes after. It is similarly the case for Matthew and Mark.

Next, Luke is thought to disagree with Matthew and Mark because he wrote that the women went to the tomb "very early in the morning" (Luke 24:1). Again, though, this time expression is similar to, if not synonymous with, those given in Matthew and Mark. In fact, the phrase could refer to anytime after midnight! "Very early in the morning" encompasses a sizeable portion of time. Luke's rendering is, therefore, compatible with Matthew and Mark.

But doesn't John most definitely contradict the others? His phrase "while it was still dark" (John 20:1), many say, is certainly not compatible with "at dawn" or "just after sunrise," when obviously it would no longer be dark. But we must consider again the normal use of language. "While it was still dark" *can* describe conditions that exist "at dawn." Everyone who has been up "at dawn" certainly knows it is not yet fully light. In fact, depending on weather conditions, it can be quite dark even at dawn or just after sunrise.

In addition, other factors indicate that there is no contradiction among the accounts. The writers may have had in mind different periods of time; the starting point could have been when the women left their houses, were traveling, or actually arrived at the tomb. Examining the Greek text, Bible scholar Gleason Archer suggests:

> The women apparently started their journey from the house in Jerusalem while it was still dark...even though it was already early morning...(John 20:1). But by the time they arrived, dawn was glimmering in the East....Mark 16:2 adds that the tip of the sun had actually appeared above the horizon.[3]

We often do not stop to consider that the women had made *a journey* to the tomb. The location of the women during their trip to the tomb would influence each author's decision about what kind of language he uses. No real grounds for a contradiction arise here.

There is an additional reason the time expressions in the four accounts may differ: Certain of the women made a delay to purchase spices (presuming that they acquired them Sunday morning rather than the evening before, after the Sabbath was over). This would have required additional time and would explain the difference between

John's Gospel and the others. In this event, Mary herself would have arrived at the tomb alone, before the other women.

John Wenham suggests there is no cause to find a contradiction here:

> There is perhaps no need to insist upon any distinction between Matthew's "toward the dawn," Mark's "very early," Luke's "early dawn" and John's "while it was still dark." Darkness and light are relative terms and it would be perfectly possible, and not inaccurate, for one person to describe the time as "early dawn" which another described as "still dark." It needs to be remembered, however, that it could have been undeniably dark on the women's departure and undeniably light on their arrival, particularly if their starting point were Bethany....We undoubtedly get a consistent and coherent picture if we see the first departures as being in the dark and the last arrivals as being before [full] sunrise.[4]

## 11. Can other alleged contradictions in the four Gospels be resolved?

Our method for attempting to resolve the various alleged contradictions among the four Gospels is to reconstruct plausible and logical sequences of events that explain the evidence and show that the accounts do not contradict. For a full discussion of other alleged contradictions, go to www.johnankerberg.org and see our article "Alleged Contradictions in the Resurrection Accounts."

# Nine Facts that Disprove *Discovery Channel's* "The Lost Tomb of Jesus"

**By Dr. John Ankerberg and Dillon Burroughs**

A t a press conference on February 26, 2007, filmmakers and researchers unveiled two ancient stone boxes they claim may have once contained the remains of Jesus and Mary Magdalene. On Sunday, March 4, 2007, "The Lost Tomb of Jesus," produced by Oscar-winning director James Cameron, aired nationwide on the *Discovery Channel*. A related book by Simcha and Charles Pellegrino, entitled *The Jesus Family Tomb: The Discovery, the Investigation, and the Evidence That Could Change History* (HarperCollins), released on the day of the press conference to coordinate with the special.

The argument is made that ten small caskets discovered in 1980 in a Jerusalem suburb may have held the bones of Jesus and his family. The researchers even claim that one of the caskets bears the title, "Judah, son of Jesus," hinting that Jesus may have had a son. But what truth can be verified in this story?

The truth is that several unsupportable assumptions have been made in relation to the alleged lost tomb of Jesus. In an effort to determine whether any of these assumptions are supported by facts, we sought the help of some qualified individuals who serve as professors and experts on Christianity in today's universities and graduate institutions. From them, we were able to put together nine facts that disprove the assumptions made in the television special and the book.

## 1. The Jesus family tomb would not have been in Jerusalem, but Nazareth.

Dr. Darrell Bock, research professor of New Testament at Dallas Theological Seminary, asks, "How did Jesus' family have the time in the aftermath of his death to buy the tomb space, while also pulling off a stealing of the body and continuing to preach that Jesus was raised *bodily*, not merely spiritually?

"The bodily part of this resurrection is key because in Judaism, when there was a belief in resurrection, it was a belief in a *bodily* resurrection—a redemption that redeemed the full scope of what God had created. If one reads 2 Maccabees 7, one will see the martyrdom of the third son of seven executed who declares that they can mutilate his tongue and hands for defending the law, because God will give them back to him one day.

"To lack a bodily resurrection teaching is to teach in distinction from what the earliest church had received as a key element of the hope that Jesus left his followers, a hope that itself was rooted in Jewish precedent. Paul, our earliest witness to testify to this in writings we possess, was a former Pharisee who held to a physical resurrection, as 1 Corinthians 15 makes clear. Paul matches the Maccabean picture noted above. He explicitly denies an approach that accepts only a spiritual resurrection."[1]

## 2. If this is the family tomb of Jesus, why does it contain so many nonfamily members?

Jesus was born in Bethlehem and his family lived in Nazareth. So it would be strange enough for his family to be buried together in

Jerusalem. But it's even stranger that the family tomb would include several nonfamily members. There is not a shred of historical evidence to account for this inconsistency.

On the contrary, the Israeli archaeologist who discovered the ancient burial caves 27 years ago says there is absolutely no proof to Cameron's outlandish claims. What's more, the archaeologist says that Cameron and his team are merely trying to profit by attacking a central tenet of the Christian faith that Jesus was raised from the dead on the third day and that his body has never been discovered.

"The claim that the burial site [of Jesus] has been found is not based on any proof, and is only an attempt to sell," says Israeli archaeologist professor Amos Kloner. A similar film was released 11 years ago, and Kloner said that this current film was merely a renewed effort to create controversy in the Christian world in order to make a bigger profit. He added, "I refute all their claims and efforts to waken a renewed interest in the findings. With all due respect, they are not archaeologists."[2]

### 3. The statistical analysis concerning Jesus is highly exaggerated. The name *Jesus* was a popular name in the first century. It has been found in 99 other tombs and on 22 other ossuaries.

The name *Jesus* was a popular first-century name, discovered on 121 other tombs and ossuaries dating from this time period. According to the details in a famous catalog of ossuary names that has been out since 2002 with the information known about this locale since c. 1980, we find:

> Out of a total number of 2,625 males, these are the figures for the ten most popular male names among Palestinian Jews. The first figure is the total number of occurrences, while the second is the number of occurrences specifically on ossuaries.
>
> | | | |
> |---|---|---|
> | 1. Simon/Simeon | 243 | 59 |
> | 2. Joseph | 218 | 45 |

| 3. Eleazar | 166 | 29 |
| 4. Judah | 164 | 44 |
| 5. John/Yohanan | 122 | 25 |
| 6. Jesus | 99 | 22 |
| 7. Hananiah | 82 | 18 |
| 8. Jonathan | 71 | 14 |
| 9. Matthew | 62 | 17 |
| 10. Manaen/Menahem | 42 | 4[3] |

This indicates that of all existing tombs and ossuaries of the period, there is nearly a 1 in 20 (4.6 percent) chance that any male tomb would have the name Jesus on it. Yet according to the statistics given in the television special, the evidence is 600 to 1 in favor of their story being true.

## 4. The statistics are also distorted regarding Mary of Magdalene.

The name *Mariamne,* a variation of *Maria,* was one of the most common names of the time. According to the details on names provided by professor Richard Bauckham of St. Andrews and sourced in a famous catalog of ossuary names that has been out since 2002 with the information known about this locale since c. 1980, we find:

> For women, we have a total of 328 occurrences (women's names are much less often recorded than men's), and figures for the 4 most popular names are thus:
>
> | 1. Mary/Mariamne | 70 | 42 |
> | 2. Salome | 58 | 41 |
> | 3. Shelamzion | 24 | 19 |
> | 4. Martha | 20 | 17[4] |

The true statistics reveal that Mary was the most common name on tombs during this time period—21 percent of Jewish women were called Mariamne (Mary). This is hardly strong evidence suggesting Mary as *the* Mary Magdalene of the New Testament.

## 5. The DNA evidence is irrelevant and untrustworthy.

In the film, reference is made to a DNA test showing that Mariamne and Jesus' DNA residues do not match. Based on that one shred of evidence, the researchers claim the couple was married and that this couple must be Jesus and Mary Magdalene. With how many women in Judea would Jesus' DNA not match? Even women named Mariamne? This proves nothing. It only states the obvious—that the two were not related, nothing more. In addition, even the DNA evidence is scientifically shaky.

According to Dr. Witherington, "There is no independent DNA control sample to compare to what was garnered from the bones in this tomb. By this I mean that the most the DNA evidence can show is that several of these folks are inter-related. Big deal. We would need an independent control sample from some member of Jesus' family to confirm that these were members of Jesus' family. We do not have that at all. In addition, mitochondrial DNA does not reveal genetic coding or XY chromosome makeup anyway. They would need nuclear DNA for that, in any case. So the DNA stuff is probably thrown in to make this look more like a real scientific fact."[5]

## 6. There is no historical evidence that Jesus was ever married or had a child.

The argument that Jesus was married or had a child comes solely from silence. No New Testament document speaks of such relationships, nor do Christian or secular writings from the early centuries of Christianity. The closest any source comes to bringing this up is the apocryphal *Gospel of Philip,* written approximately A.D. 275, written neither by the apostle nor in the time period of the New Testament. As our book *The Da Vinci Code Controversy*[6] notes, even the passage used to suggest a married Jesus is used grossly out of context.

## 7. There is no historical evidence that connects Mariamne and Mary Magdalene.

To get Mariamne to match Mary Magdalene rather than one of numerous other Marys of that day, a researcher would need to find historical information that notes such a connection. The closest the film special comes to providing such evidence is based on a fourth-century manuscript known as the apocryphal Acts. This very work itself is not based on historical fact and dates much later than the actual events its notes. In the end, we have no compelling reason to believe the Mariamne of the so-called "family tomb" is Mary Magdalene, a claim that stands as a key point for the entire production.

## 8. The trouble with James, the brother of Jesus, is history says he was buried alone in another tomb.

Eusebius, Christianity's earliest historian (fourth century), recorded that there had been a tomb of James the Just, the brother of Jesus, known in Jerusalem since New Testament times. Its location was near the Temple Mount and had an honoric stele next to it. The spot was known as a pilgrimage site for many Christians.

"It was apparently a single tomb, with no other holy family members mentioned nor any other ossuaries in that place," states Dr. Witherington. "The locality and singularity of this tradition rules out a family tomb in Talpiot. Christians would not have been making pilgrimage to the tomb if they believed Jesus' bones were in it—that would have contradicted and violated their faith, but the bones of holy James were another matter. They were consider sacred relics."

This is clearly not in Talpiot, and remember, to claim there is a Talpiot family tomb means that Jesus would have been buried there long before James was martyred in A.D. 62. In other words, the James tradition contradicts the Talpiot tomb both in locale and in substance. James is buried alone, in a completely different place.

## 9. There is multiple historical attestation that both Christians and non-Christians knew where the tomb of Jesus was, and that it was found empty on the third day.

Dr. Ben Witherington, professor of New Testament at Asbury Seminary and author of *What Have They Done with Jesus?* notes: "By all ancient accounts, the tomb of Jesus was empty—even the Jewish and Roman authorities acknowledged this. Now it takes a year for the flesh to desiccate, and then you put the man's bones in an ossuary. But Jesus' body was long gone from Joseph of Arimathea's tomb well before then. Are we really to believe it was moved to another tomb, decayed, and then was put in an ossuary? It's not likely.

"Implicitly you must accuse James, Peter, and John (mentioned in Galatians 1–2 in our earliest New Testament document from A.D. 49) of fraud and coverup. Are we really to believe that they knew Jesus didn't rise bodily from the dead but perpetrated a fraudulent religion for which they and others were prepared to die? Did they really hide the body of Jesus in another tomb? We need to remember that the James in question is Jesus' brother, who certainly would have known about a family tomb. This frankly is impossible for me to believe."[7]

According to Bock, we have to "accept that as they scrambled to steal the body they were yet preaching an empty tomb and resurrection when they actually knew that Jesus was not raised. They had to secretly buy the tomb space from someone, prepare an ossuary over a year's period, and then choose to adorn the ossuary of Jesus with graffiti-like script to name their dead hero. Surely if they had a year to prepare for honoring Jesus, they would have adorned his ossuary with more than a mere graffiti-like inscription. Not to mention that some of the family died for this belief, when they really knew Jesus had not left the tomb empty. This scenario seems quite implausible."[8]

Dr. Stephen Pfann, a biblical scholar at the University of the Holy Land in Jerusalem, who was interviewed in the documentary, said the film's hypothesis holds little weight.

"I don't think that Christians are going to buy into this," he said.

"But skeptics, in general, would like to see something that pokes holes into the story that so many people hold dear."

Dr. Pfann is even unsure that the name *Jesus* on the caskets was read correctly. He thinks it's more likely the name *Hanun*. Ancient Semitic script is notoriously difficult to decipher. [9]

William Dever, an expert on Near Eastern archaeology and anthropology, who has worked with Israeli archaeologists for five decades, said specialists have known about the ossuaries for years. "The fact that it's been ignored tells you something....It [the film] would be amusing if it didn't mislead so many people."[10]

Should we be concerned about "The Lost Tomb of Jesus?" Yes. Christians should be bothered that others would speak of the Jesus we worship as anything less than God's divine Son. And non-Christians should be bothered that assumptions would be presented seemingly as "proofs" without taking the time to examine what we do and do not know to be fact. But should we be worried? No. The "evidence" fails to prove anything other than the fact that controversy about Jesus continues to draw attention.

For Christians, the challenge is to know the truth of God's Word and to continue to communicate it to others through our actions and words. As Dr. Bock noted, "Hopefully our times have not slid to the point where we can no longer tell the difference between Jerusalem and Hollywood."[11]

# Discussion Guide

These discussion questions are intended to facilitate further conversation between friends or members of small groups, book clubs, and church groups. Please feel free to use them in whatever way helps you best grapple with the issues shared in this book. Greater understanding often results from the conversation itself rather than simply the bottom-line answer. For additional perspectives or other helpful resources, please see the "Additional Resources" section in this book or check out any of the numerous articles, audio, or video tools available at www.johnankerberg.org.

## Why Should I Care About Jesus?

- What are some of the reasons people don't care about Jesus?

- On a scale of 1 to 10, how deeply are you personally concerned about better understanding who Jesus is?

- If someone asked you, "Why should I spend my time learning anything about Jesus?" how would you respond?

## Part One: What Do We *Really* Know About Jesus?

1. The Biographies of Jesus: What Did His Friends Say?

- What parts of the four Gospels have you read? What was your initial reaction to these accounts?

- Why do you think there are four different Gospels? How is each one unique?

- If someone asked you, "What do the Gospels say about Jesus that has relevance for my life today?" what would you say?

2. The Media of Jesus: What Did Others Say About Him?

- How does outside information about the life of Jesus help affirm the reliability of the words in the New Testament?

- Why are the early church fathers important in our understanding of Jesus?

- In what ways do words from enemies of Christ and Christianity in early Christian history help affirm what we know about Jesus?

3. The World of Jesus: What Does His Culture Tell Us About Him?

- Which of the archaeological discoveries shared in this chapter best help affirm what you believe about Jesus? Which is of least importance?

- How does the discovery of historical locations cited in the New Testament affirm the reliability of what the New Testament books say?

- What are the potential dangers in relying too heavily on outside artifacts to "prove" events from the Bible?

4. The Accounts of Jesus: How Reliable Are the Manuscripts We Have Today?

- How does an evaluation of various early copies of the New Testament help affirm a person's belief in Jesus?

- Based on the information regarding the New Testament's transmission, how important do you believe it is for people to investigate the New Testament's development as part of their spiritual growth?

- In what ways could you respond to a person who claims that the New Testament is full of errors?

## Part Two: Who Did Jesus Claim to Be?

5. The Miracles of Jesus: Did He Really Perform Supernatural Acts?

- What attitudes do your friends have about miracles?

- In what ways can science and extrabiblical research strengthen the claim that Jesus performed miracles?

- How could you share about the importance of miracles to someone who believes miracles do not occur?

6. The Claims of Jesus: Did He Really Believe He Was God's Son?

- Which of the three passages from John do you feel provides the clearest insight into Jesus' claim to be God?

- How do the words of those who opposed Jesus reveal his claim to be divine?

- In what ways does the claim of Jesus being divine influence how we should live our lives today?

7. The Thinking of Jesus: Was He Just Making Up This Stuff?

- In what ways did Jesus' enemies attempt to discredit what he taught about being God's son?

- How do Jesus' actions show that he was not a liar or a sincerely misguided individual?

- In what ways does the classic discussion of deciding whether Jesus is Lord, liar, or lunatic help in understanding Jesus? In what ways can this approach be unhelpful?

8. The Prophecies of Jesus: Did His Life Really Fulfill the Predictions?

- How does affirming Jesus as the fulfillment of Old Testament predictions show that he is God's son?
- Which of the prophecies listed in this chapter is the most compelling to you?
- If someone claimed that Jesus' fulfillment of prophecy was only coincidental, how could you respond?

## Part Three: Did Jesus Really Come Alive Again?

9. The Death of Jesus: What Does the Medical Evidence Suggest?

- How valuable do you feel the medical evaluations of Jesus' death are to your understanding of his death?
- What limitations do you see in evaluating the death of Jesus from a distance?
- Why does an affirmation of Jesus' death stand as such a critical part of the resurrection of Jesus and the Christian faith?

10. The Burial of Jesus: How Was He Buried?

- How strong do you feel the evidence is for the traditional burial of Jesus?
- Why do some people suggest different versions of Jesus' burial?
- In what ways is the burial of Jesus a critical historical fact in showing the big deal about Jesus' resurrection?

11. The Empty Tomb of Jesus: Where Did His Body Go?

- In what ways would the enemies of Jesus have been able to prove he was still dead after others claimed Jesus was alive?

- Why was there so much of a cover-up by the Jews and Romans about the disappearance of Jesus' body?

- How could you respond to a person who claimed Jesus' body had been taken by his followers?

12. The Appearances of Jesus: Did People Really See Him Alive after His Death?

- What was the significance of Jesus first appearing to women?

- In what ways was the postresurrection body of Jesus different from his earlier body? How was it the same?

- How could you respond to people who claim the resurrection is simply a legend?

13. The Followers of Jesus: Did His Friends Believe He Was Alive?

- How does learning about the lives of Jesus' apostles after Jesus' death and resurrection strengthen the argument that Jesus did rise from the dead?

- What can a person do to have a relationship with Jesus today?

Conclusion: What Should I Do with Jesus?

- What is the consensus of the scholars who are quoted in this chapter—what do they say our attitude toward Jesus should be?

- Where do you stand in relation to Jesus? Did you pray the prayer found in this section? If so, who can you tell about your decision?

- What are the top two or three benefits you have received from time reading *What's the Big Deal About Jesus?* How will this book change your attitude or actions?

# Additional Resources

Interested in learning more? If you are serious about reading more on the life of Christ and the Christian faith, several excellent tools are available. We have listed below several resources from The Ankerberg Theological Research Institute as well as some helpful Web sites. **Please note** that this does not mean we agree with all the resources found at those sites.

## Ankerberg Theological Research Institute Resources

All of the following Ankerberg resources can be ordered online at www.johnankerberg.org or by phone at (423) 892-7722.

*Books*

All the following books are authored or coauthored by Dr. John Ankerberg:

*Ready with An Answer for the Tough Questions About God* (Eugene, OR: Harvest House, 1997)

*The Passion and the Empty Tomb: The Case for the Resurrection of Jesus* (Eugene, OR: Harvest House, 2004)

*The Case for Jesus the Messiah: Incredible Prophecies that Prove God Exists* (Chattanooga, TN: Ankerberg Theological Research Institute, 1989)

*Do the Resurrection Accounts Conflict? And What Proof Is There That Jesus Rose from the Dead?* (Chattanooga, TN: Ankerberg Theological Research Institute, 1990)

*Fast Facts on Defending Your Faith* (Eugene, OR: Harvest House, 2002)

*The Facts on Why You Can Believe the Bible* (Eugene, OR: Harvest House, 2004)

*The Facts on the Jesus Seminar* (Eugene, OR: Harvest House, 1997)

*The Facts on Jesus the Messiah* (Eugene, OR: Harvest House, 1993)

*Knowing the Truth About the Reliability of the Bible* (Eugene, OR: Harvest House, 1997)

*Knowing the Truth About the Resurrection* (Eugene, OR: Harvest House, 1996)

*Knowing the Truth About Jesus the Messiah* (Eugene, OR: Harvest House, 1996)


*Video Programs and Transcripts*

The following topics are available in VHS and DVD formats. Most of the programs also have downloadable transcripts available.

*Did Jesus Rise from the Dead?* (Plus Q&A Session)

*Did the Resurrection Really Happen?*

*Do Fulfilled Messianic Prophecies in the Old Testament Constitute Proof that God Exists and that Jesus Is God's Messiah?*

*Do the Messianic Prophecies in the Old Testament Clearly Point to Jesus Christ or Somebody Else?*

*Four Historical Facts that Prove Jesus Really Rose from the Dead*

*From Skepticism to Belief—The Facts and Evidence that Can Lead You Step by Step to Belief in Christ*

*If Jesus Wasn't God, Then He Deserved an Oscar*

*Is Christianity Based on Fact or Fantasy?*

*Refuting the New Controversial Theories About Jesus*

*The Claims of Jesus Christ*

*The Evidence for the Historical Jesus*

*The Search for Jesus Continues*

*Was Jesus Christ a Liar, a Lunatic, a Legend, or God?*

*What About the Missing Gospels and Lost Christianities?*

*What Proof Exists that Jesus Rose from the Dead?*

## Online Articles

Over 2,500 online articles on Christianity and comparative religions are hosted on The Ankerberg Theological Research Institute Web site. For those dealing specifically with apologetics, see the link http://www.johnankerberg.org/Articles/archives-ap.htm.

## Helpful Web Sites

Here are some of the Web sites we have found helpful for studying about Jesus and Christianity:

www.christianitytoday.com: *Christianity Today* magazine offers articles and Bible studies from a Christian perspective.

www.sermoncentral.com: Provides sermon transcripts and notes for preachers and other teachers.

www.leaderu.com: A ministry of Campus Crusade for Christ, LeaderU offers links and articles on Christianity, ranging from entry level to academic.

www.bible.org: Home of the NET Bible, this site offers thousands of articles on nearly every aspect of Bible study.

www.biblegateway.com: Search the major English translations of the Bible by passage, keyword, or topic.

www.probe.org: A Christian media ministry that offers numerous online articles and audio resources on Christianity and culture.

www.trueu.org: A Focus on the Family Web site for college-age individuals which provides articles on defending the Christian faith.

# Notes

## Why Should I Care About Jesus?

1. For more information on this issue, see Dillon Burroughs, *The Jesus Family Tomb Controversy: How the Evidence Falls Short* (Ann Arbor, MI: Nimble Books, 2007).

2. "ACLU, People for the American Way Join Forces to Oppose Rutherford Institute Lawsuit Over City Council Member's Right to Pray 'in Jesus' Name,'" The Rutherford Institute press release, February 22, 2006. Accessed at http://rutherford.org/articles_db/press_release.asp?article_id=600.

## Chapter 1—The Biographies of Jesus

1. Marcus Borg, *Meeting Jesus Again for the First Time* (San Francisco, CA: HarperSanFrancisco, 1995).

2. Mark 16:15.

3. Acts 2:5.

4. Acts 2:42.

5. Acts 2:9-10.

6. Acts 5:14.

7. Acts 6:7.

8. Luke 1:1-4.

9. N.T. Wright, in an interview on "A Response to ABC's the Search for Jesus," on *The John Ankerberg Show,* 2001.

10. Romans 1:8.

11. James 1:1.

12. 1 Peter 1:1.

13. J. Ed Komoszewski, M. James Sawyer, and Daniel B. Wallace, *Reinventing Jesus* (Grand Rapids, MI: Kregel Publications, 2006), p. 30.

14. Interview with *Christianity Today,* January 18, 1963. Accessed at http://www.cvc.tv/resources/3_10ReasonsToTrustTheBible.pdf.

15. Ben Witherington, in an interview on "A Response to ABC's the Search for Jesus," on *The John Ankerberg Show,* 2001.

16. 1 Corinthians 15:3-8,11.

17. See Galatians 1–2.

18. A.N. Sherwin-White, *Roman Society and Roman Law in the New Testament* (Oxford: Clarendon Press, 1963), pp. 189–90.

19. William Lane Craig, in an interview on "A Response to ABC's the Search for Jesus," on *The John Ankerberg Show,* 2001.

20. This is traditionally called *inerrancy,* an important Christian doctrine. A fuller explanation of this concept can be found in John Ankerberg and John Weldon's *The Facts on Why You Can Believe the Bible* (Eugene, OR: Harvest House, 2004).

## Chapter 2—The Media of Jesus

1. Gary Habermas, *The Historical Jesus* (Joplin, MO: College Press, 1996), p. 250.

2. Julius Africanus, *Extant Writings,* XVIII in the Ante-Nicene Fathers, ed. by Alexander Roberts and James Donaldson (Grand Rapids, MI: Eerdmans, 1973), vol. VI, p. 130.

3. Pliny, *Letters,* trans. by William Melmoth, rev. by W.M.L. Hutchinson (Cambridge, MA: Harvard University Press, 1935), vol. II, Book X: 96.

4. Moses Hadas, *The Complete Works of Tacitus* (New York: Random House, 1942), pp. IX, XIII-XIV.

5. Ibid., 15.44.

6. Suetonius, *Claudius,* 25 (emphasis added).

7. Suetonius, *Nero,* 16 (emphasis added).

8. Lucian, "The Death of Peregrine," 11-13, in *The Works of Lucian of Samosata,* trans. H.W. Fowler and F.G. Fowler, 4 vols. (Oxford: Clarendon, 1949), vol. 4.

9. The quotes by Galen can be viewed online at http://www.earlychristianwritings.com/galen.html.

10. The quotes and sources for these writers can be found online at http://www.rationalchristianity.net/jesus_extrabib.html.

11. See all the relevant excerpts from Celsus at http://www.bluffton.edu/~humanities/1/celsus.htm.

12. Cited at http://www.rationalchristianity.net/jesus_extrabib.html.

13. Craig Blomberg, in an interview on "A Response to ABC's the Search for Jesus," on *The John Ankerberg Show,* 2001.

14. Complete citation of the church fathers in this section can be obtained at www.ankerberg.com/Articles/historical-Jesus/DaVinci/HJ-davinci-crash-davinci-code.htm#IS%20THE%20BIBLE%20AN%20UNRELIABLE%20DOCUMENT.

15. Tim LaHaye and Jerry Jenkins, *John's Story* (New York: Putnam Praise, 2006).

16. Colossians 4:12-13.

17. 1 Clement 36:1.

18. Ignatius, *Letter to the Ephesians,* 20:1.

19. Inside flap of *The Gospel of Thomas* by Marvin Meyer (San Francisco, CA: HarperSanFrancisco, 2002).

20. "Discerning Fact from Fiction in *The Da Vinci Code.*" Accessed at http://www.evidenceandanswers.com.

## Chapter 3—The World of Jesus

1. Ron Rhodes, *Answering the Objections of Atheists, Agnostics, & Skeptics* (Eugene, OR: Harvest House Publishers, 2006), p. 130.

2. Craig Evans, in an interview on "A Response to ABC's the Search for Jesus," on *The John Ankerberg Show,* 2001.

3. The following interview quotes in this chapter, unless otherwise noted, come from the program series, "A Response to ABC's the Search for Jesus," on *The John Ankerberg Show,* 2001.

4. John McRay, *Archaeology & the New Testament* (Grand Rapids, MI: Baker Book House, 2003), p. 156.

5. Eric Svendson, "Jesus' Infancy Outside of Matthew and Luke," *New Testament Research Ministries,* Novemeber 15, 2005. Accessed at http://ntrminblog.blogspot.com/2005/11/jesus-infancy-outside-of-matthew-and_15.html.

6. D.S. Pfann, in an interview on "Questions Surrounding Jesus' Birth," on *The John Ankerberg Show,* 2001.

7. Darrell Bock, in an interview on "A Response to ABC's the Search for Jesus," on *The John Ankerberg Show,* 2001.

8. D.S. Pfann, in an interview on "A Response to ABC's the Search for Jesus," on *The John Ankerberg Show,* 2001.

9. John 1:46 NASB.

10. Luke 1:26.

11. Matthew 2:23; 13:54; Luke 2:4,51; 4:16.

12. Magen Broshi, in an interview on "A Response to ABC's the Search for Jesus," on *The John Ankerberg Show,* 2001.

13. That Jesus would be called a Nazarene is traditionally considered a fulfillment of prophecy in the sense that Jesus would come from a place considered despised or of poor reputation, such as described in Isaiah 53:3 and Psalm 22:6.

14. "Jacob's Well," at ChristianAnswers.net. Accessed at http://www.christiananswers.net/dictionary/jacobswell.html.

15. John 4:29.

16. W. Hal Harris III, "Exegetical Commentary on John 4," *Biblical Studies Foundation.* Accessed at http://www.bible.org/page.php?page_id=1309.

17. "Shechem," ChristianAnswers.net. Accessed at http://www.christian answers.net/dictionary/shechem.html.

18. Mark 1:22.

19. Mark 1:21-27.

20. Luke 7:3.

21. John 6:35-59. Further details can be found at http://www.allaboutar chaeology.org/synagogue-at-capernaum-faq.htm.

22. Their site can be found at http://198.62.75.1/www1/ofm/sites/TScpsyn1.html.

23. "Capernaum—Location Profile," Ancient Sandals. Accessed at http://www.ancientsandals.com/overviews/capernaum.htm.

24. Jean Gilman, "Jerusalem Burial Cave Reveals: Names, Testimonies of First Christians," *Jerusalem Christian Review,* Internet Edition, Issue 2, Volume 9.

25. Robin M. Jenson, "The Raising of Lazarus," *Biblical Archaeology Review.* Accessed at http://members.bib-arch.org/nph-proxy.pl/000000A/http/www.basarchive.org/bswbSearch.asp=3fPubID=3dBSBR&Volume=3 d11&Issue=3d2&ArticleID=3d6&UserID=3d0&.

26. Rusty Russell, "The Pilate Inscription," at Bible History Online. Accessed at http://www.bible-history.com/empires/pilate.html.

27. Ibid.

28. Darrell Bock, in an interview on "Questions Surrounding *The Passion of the Christ,*" on *The John Ankerberg Show,* 2004.

29.  For further details, see http://www.forumancientcoins.com/Roman-Coins.asp?e=Pontius_Pilate&par=932&pos=1&target=105.

30.  Craig Evans, in an interview on "A Response to ABC's the Search for Jesus," on *The John Ankerberg Show,* 2001.

## Chapter 4—The Accounts of Jesus

1.  Marcus Borg, *Meeting Jesus Again for the First Time* (San Francisco, CA: Harper San Francisco, 1995).

2.  2 Peter 3:16.

3.  Norman Geisler, "The Canonicity of the Bible—Part Two," *Ankerberg Theological Research Institue.* Accessed at http://www.johnankerberg. org/Articles/_PDFArchives/theological-dictionary/TD3W0402.pdf.

4.  Some have even found a special significance of seven sources if Paul is considered the author of Hebrews and Mark's Gospel is included as associated with Peter.

5.  Bart Ehrman, *Misquoting Jesus* (San Francisco, CA: HarperCollins, 2005), p. 208. For an evangelical response, see *Misquotes in Misquoting Jesus* by Dillon Burroughs (Ann Arbor, MI: Nimble Books, 2006), or *Reinventing Jesus* by J. Ed Komoszewski, M. James Sawyer, and Daniel B. Wallace (Grand Rapids: Kregel, 2006).

6.  Frederic Kenyon, *The Bible and Archaeology* (New York: Harper & Brothers, 1940), p. 288.

7.  B.F. Westcott, and F.J.A. Hort, eds., *New Testament in Original Greek,* 1881, vol. II, p. 2.

8.  Bruce Metzger, *The Text of the New Testament* (Oxford: Oxford University Press, 1964; rev. ed. 1992), p. 34.

9.  From the article "If Jesus Wasn't God, Then He Deserved an Oscar, Part 3," *Ankerberg Theological Research Institute.* Accessed at http://www. johnankerberg.org/Articles/apologetics/AP0701W3.htm.

10.  Some figures cited are as high as 200,000. We have used the most common number cited in the literature.

11.  Adapted from Ron Rhodes, "Manuscript Support for the Bible's Reliability," accessed at http://home.earthlink.net/~ronrhodes/ Manuscript.html.

12.  Of course, such suggestions are not without critics. For an online discussion, see http://www.preteristarchive.com/Books/1996_thiede_ eyewitness.html. The main book on this theory is *Eyewitness to Jesus* by Carsten Peter Thiede and Matthew D'Ancona (New York: Doubleday, 1996).

13.  John Warwick Montgomery, in an interview on "Lord, Liar, or Lunatic" on *The John Ankerberg Show,* 1987.

# Chapter 5—The Miracles of Jesus

1. Marcus J. Borg, *Jesus, A New Vision: Spirit, Culture, and the Life of Discipleship* (San Francisco, CA: HarperSanFrancisco, 1991), p. 61.

2. Cited at http://www.christiantrumpetsounding.com/heavens_declare. htm.

3. Interview quotes in this chapter are all from "A Response to ABC's the Search for Jesus," on *The John Ankerberg Show,* 2001.

4. "Q," *Biblical Studies Foundation.* Accessed at http://www.read-the-bible. org/glossary.html#Q.

5. Norman Geisler, "Questions About Miracles—Part Five," *Ankerberg Theological Research Institute.* Accessed at http://www.johnankerberg. org/Articles/_PDFArchives/theological-dictionary/TD3W0300.pdf.

6. "Some Well-Known Miracles of Jesus," at Bible Resource Center. Accessed online at http://www.bibleresourcecenter.org/vsItemDisplay. dsp&objectID=F38BB037-BFF6-47FE-A828BEA35B562AE8&method od=display.

7. As quoted in the *International Standard Bible Encyclopedia* (Grand Rapids: Eerdmans, 1939), p. 2036.

# Chapter 6—The Claims of Jesus

1. John 14:6.

2. John 6:26-40.

3. Matthew 9:2.

4. Matthew 10:32 (emphasis added).

5. Matthew 24:36 (emphasis added).

6. Gary Habermas, in an interview on "Is the Jesus of History the Jesus of Faith?" on *The John Ankerberg Show,* 2000.

7. Matthew 5–7.

8. Matthew 5:27-28.

9. Matthew 7:29.

10. Mark 14:61-62.

11. Stephen used it in reference to Jesus in Acts 7:56, and the apostle John in Revelation 1:13.

12. Daniel 7:13-14 (emphasis added).

13. John 8:52-53 NLT (emphasis added).

14. John 8:56 NLT.

15. John 8:58 NLT.

16. John 8:59 NLT.

17. John 10:24 NLT.

18. John 10:25-30 NLT (emphasis added).

19. John 10:31-33 NLT (emphasis added).

20. Claire Pfann, in an interview on "A Response to ABC's the Search for Jesus," on *The John Ankerberg Show, 2001.*

21. Craig Evans, in an interview on "A Response to ABC's the Search for Jesus," on *The John Ankerberg Show, 2001.*

22. John 14:6 NLT.

23. John 14:9-10 NLT (emphasis added).

24. A special thanks to the booklet *Who Is This Man Who Says He Is God?* by RBC Ministries. Available online at http://www.rbc.org/uploadedFiles/Bible_Study/Discovery_Series/PDFs/Who_Is_This_Man_Who_Says_He's_God.pdf.

25. Matthew 21:13 NLT.

26. This chart has been adapted from Matthew J. Slick, "God Cannot Be Tempted," *CARM Resources.* Accessed at http://www.carm.org/doctrine/obj_Jesus_sin.htm.

27. Matthew 21:16 NLT.

28. Matthew 16:13 NLT.

29. Matthew 16:15 NLT (emphasis added).

30. Matthew 16:16 NLT.

31. *Who Is This Man Who Says He Is God?* (Grand Rapids, MI: RBC Ministries, 2002), p. 20.

32. Matthew 16:17 NLT.

33. John 20:25 NLT.

34. John 20:26-28 NLT.

35. John 20:29 NLT.

36. C.S. Lewis, *Mere Christianity,* quoted at the C.S. Lewis Web site http://cslewis.drzeus.net/papers/mere.html.

37. Matthew 4:10 NLT, quoted from Deuteronomy 6:13.

38. Matthew 28:16-17 NLT.

39. Matthew 28:17 NLT.

## Chapter 7—The Thinking of Jesus

1. David Reinhard, "Jesus of Nazareth: Lord or Lunatic?" *The Oregonian.* Cited online at http://atheism.about.com/b/a/014615.htm.

2. Cited in Josh McDowell, "The Trilemma: Lord, Liar, or Lunatic?"

Accessed at http://www.greatcom.org/resources/areadydefense/ch21/default.htm.

3. Adapted from the excellent outline "Was Jesus a Lunatic?" found at http://www.geocities.com/FaithInEvidence/luna.html.

4. Mark 3:20-21.

5. Pat Zukeran, "The Uniqueness of Jesus," at Leadership University. Accessed at http://www.leaderu.com/orgs/probe/docs/unique.html.

6. Matthew 7:28-29.

7. 1 Corinthians 15:5-8 (emphasis added).

8. Mark 3:22. A similar passage is found in John 10:20.

9. "Was Jesus a Lunatic?" Accessed at http://www.geocities.com/FaithIn-Evidence/luna.html.

10. Luke 22:70-71 (emphasis added).

11. Philip Schaff, *The Person of Christ* (New York: American Tract Society, 1918), p. 97.

12. Matthew 9:36 (emphasis added).

13. Matthew 14:14 (emphasis added).

14. Matthew 15:32 (emphasis added).

15. Matthew 20:34 (emphasis added).

16. Mark 1:40-41 (emphasis added).

17. Mark 6:34 (emphasis added).

18. Mark 8:2 (emphasis added).

19. Matthew 8:27 (emphasis added).

20. Matthew 9:33 (emphasis added).

21. Matthew 15:31 (emphasis added).

22. Mark 2:12 (emphasis added).

23. Mark 6:51 (emphasis added).

24. Mark 12:17 (emphasis added).

25. Luke 4:22 (emphasis added).

26. Luke 9:42-43 (emphasis added).

27. Luke 11:14 (emphasis added).

28. Lee Strobel, *The Case for Christ* (Grand Rapids, MI: Zondervan, 1998), p. 146.

## Chapter 8—The Prophecies of Jesus

1. John Ankerberg and Walter C. Kaiser, *The Case for Jesus the Messiah* (Chattanooga, TN: The John Ankerberg Evangelism Association, 1989), p. 16.

2. John Ankerberg, John Weldon, and Walter Kaiser, *The Case for Jesus the Messiah* (Melbourne: Pacific College Study Series, 1994), pp. 17-18.

3. Genesis 3:14-15.

4. Genesis 9:19,26-27.

5. Genesis 49:1,8.

6. Deuteronomy 18:15.

7. 2 Samuel 7:2-5,11,16.

8. Isaiah 7:14; 9:6.

9. Micah 5:2.

10. Isaiah 40:3.

11. Psalm 22; Isaiah 53.

12. Daniel 9:24-27.

13. Isaiah 53.

14. Isaiah 53:4-5,8-9,12.

15. Zechariah 12:10.

16. Zechariah 11:12-13.

17. Isaiah 53:8-9.

18. Psalm 22:16.

19. Zechariah 12:10.

20. Isaiah 53:9.

21. Psalm 16:10.

22. Pat Zukeran, "The Uniqueness of Jesus," at Leadership University. Accessed online at http://www.leaderu.com/orgs/probe/docs/unique.html.

23. Alfred Edersheim, *The Life and Times of Jesus the Messiah,* one volume edition (Grand Rapids, MI: Eerdmans, 1972), p. 163. You can also view all 456 of these prophecies at http://www.levendwater.org/books/life_times_edersheim_appendix.pdf, pp. 59ff.

24. Emile Borel, *Probabilities and Life,* M. Baudin, trans. (New York: Dover, 1962), p. 28.

25. Micah 5:2.

26. Matthew 2:1.

27. Matthew 2:5.

28. Genesis 49:10.

29. Matthew 1:1-16; Luke 3:23-37.

30. Isaiah 40:3.

31. Matthew 3:1-2.

32. Zechariah 9:9.

33. Psalm 41:9.

34. Matthew 26:47-50.

35. Matthew 26:14-16.

36. Zechariah 11:4.

37. Zechariah 11:12 (emphasis added).

38. Exodus 21:32.

39. Isaiah 49:3ff.

40. Isaiah 50:6.

41. Matthew 26:67-68 (emphasis added).

42. Matthew 27:28-30 (emphasis added).

43. Isaiah 53:5.

44. Matthew 27:26.

45. Matthew 27:12-14.

46. Isaiah 53:7.

47. Zechariah 11:13.

48. Matthew 27:3-5 NLT.

49. Matthew 27:6-8 (emphasis added).

50. Psalm 22:16.

51. Luke 23:33.

52. Psalm 59:6.

53. Isaiah 53:12 (emphasis added).

54. Matthew 27:38.

## Part Three: Did Jesus Really Come Alive Again?

1. Edwin Yamauchi, in the interview "Are Christians Intolerant to Claim Jesus Is the Only Way?" on *The John Ankerberg Show,* 2001.

2. Craig Evans, in the interview "Are Christians Intolerant to Claim Jesus Is the Only Way?" on *The John Ankerberg Show,* 2001.

3. 1 Corinthians 15:14,19 (emphasis added).

4. All interview quotes in this chapter, unless otherwise noted, are adapted from interview transcripts of "Are Christians Intolerant to Claim Jesus Is the Only Way?" on *The John Ankerberg Show,* 2001.

5. Matthew 26:17–27:61; Mark 14:12–15:47; Luke 22:7–23:56; John 13:1–19:42.

6. David Watson, *Jesus Then and Now* (Belleville, MI: Lion, 1986), p. 5.

7. M. Hengel, *Crucifixion in the Ancient World and the Folly of the Message of the Cross,* J. Bowden, trans. (Philadelphia, PA: Fortress Press, 1977), pp. 22-45, 86-90.

8. Although exceptions were made to scourge Roman soldiers who defected from service.

9. R. Bucklin, "The Legal and Medical Aspects of the Trial and Death of Christ," *Science Law,* 1970; 10:14-26.

10. P. Barbet, *A Doctor at Calvary: The Passion of Our Lord Jesus Christ as Described by a Surgeon,* Earl of Wicklow, trans. (Garden City, NY: Doubleday Image Books, 1953), pp. 12-18, 37-147, 159-75, 187-208.

11. "Scourging," article accessed at http://the-crucifixion.org/scourging.htm#11#11.

12. C. Truman Davis, "A Physician Analyzes the Crucifixion," *New Wine Magazine,* April 1982. Accessed at http://the-crucifixion.org/jesus/physician.html.

13. Ibid.

14. From http://the-crucifixion.org/.

15. L. Michael White, professor of classics and director of the religious studies program at University of Texas at Austin, during a PBS interview. Accessed at http://www.pbs.org/wgbh/pages/frontline/shows/religion/jesus/arrest.html.

16. See the image at http://www.pbs.org/wgbh/pages/frontline/shows/religion/jesus/crucifixion.html.

17. Thanks to the article "Crucifixion" for many of the concepts utilized in this section. Accessed at http://www.frugalsites.net/jesus/crucifixion.htm.

18. C. Truman Davis, "A Physician Analyzes the Crucifixion," *New Wine Magazine,* April 1982. Accessed online at http://the-crucifixion.org/jesus/physician.html.

19. S.M. Tenney, "On Death by Crucifixion," *American Heart Journal,* 1964; 68:286-87.

20. John 19:34.

21. C. Truman Davis, "A Physician Analyzes the Crucifixion," *New Wine Magazine,* April 1982. Accessed online at http://the-crucifixion.org/jesus/physician.html.

22. Norman L. Geisler, *Baker Dictionary of Christian Apologetics* (Grand Rapids, MI: Baker Books, 1998), p. 128.

23. J.H. Charlesworth, "Jesus and Jehohanon: Archaeological Notes on Crucifixion," *The Expository Times,* February 1973, vol. IXXXIV, no. 6. Accessed at http://www.pbs.org/wgbh/pages/frontline/shows/religion/jesus/crucifixion.html.

## Chapter 10–The Burial of Jesus

1. John MacArthur, "The Amazing Burial of Jesus," sermon transcript GC 2399. Accessed at http://www.biblebb.com/files/MAC/2399.HTM.
2. Mark 15:42-46.
3. Mark 16:4.
4. See John 19:38-42.
5. Hall Harris III, *John 19: Exegetical Commentary* at http://www.bible.org/page.php?page_id=2715.
6. Mark 16:1; Luke 24:1.

## Chapter 11–The Empty Tomb of Jesus

1. Dr. William Lane Craig in M. Wilkins and J.P. Moreland, editors, *Jesus Under Fire* (Grand Rapids, MI: Zondervan, 1995), p. 149.
2. Paul Althaus in Wolfhart Pannenberg, *Jesus—God and Man* (London: SCM Press, 1968), p. 100.
3. All interview quotes in this chapter, unless otherwise noted, are adapted from interview transcripts of "Are Christians Intolerant to Claim Jesus Is the Only Way?" on *The John Ankerberg Show,* 2001.
4. "The Disciples Stole Jesus' Body and Faked His Resurrection," CARM Resources. Accessed at http://www.carm.org/evidence/faked resurrection.htm.
5. Matthew 28:11-15 NASB.
6. Cited by Josh McDowell, "Evidence for the Resurrection." Accessed at http://www.leaderu.com/everystudent/easter/articles/josh2.html.
7. N.T. Wright, in an interview on "A Response to ABC's the Search for Jesus," on *The John Ankerberg Show,* 2001.
8. Acts 2:32.

## Chapter 12–The Appearances of Jesus

1. N.T. Wright, in an interview on "A Response to ABC's the Search for Jesus," on *The John Ankerberg Show,* 2001. Interview quotes in this chapter are all from this show.
2. Cover image available at http://www.answers.com/topic/elvis-sightings.
3. "Elvis Sightings." Accessed at http://en.wikipedia.org/wiki/Elvis_sightings. Also see http://www.elvissightingbulletinboard.com.
4. Acts 7:54-56.
5. Mark 16:9; see also John 20:15-28.

6. Mark 16:1.

7. Matthew 28:9-10.

8. Other supernatural events do occur, such as the angels at the tomb, the removal of the rock from the tomb entrance, and the reaction of the guards at the tomb. However, our focus in this chapter is on the actual sightings themselves.

9. Luke 24:30-31,33. Also found in Mark 16:12-13.

10. See Luke 24:33-34; 1 Corinthians 15:5.

11. 1 Corinthians 15:4-5.

12. Luke 24:36-43. Also found in John 20:19-23.

13. John 20:24-25.

14. John 20:26-28.

15. John 21:4-7.

16. 1 Corinthians 15:6.

17. George Konig, "The Resurrection Appearances of Jesus." Accessed at http://www.konig.org/wc26.htm.

18. 1 Corinthians 15:7.

19. Matthew 13:55.

20. Acts 12:17.

21. John 7:5.

22. Acts 12:17; 15:13; 21:18.

23. Darrell Bock, in an interview on "A Response to ABC's the Search for Jesus," on *The John Ankerberg Show,* 2001.

24. Matthew 28:16-17.

25. Matthew 28:19-20.

26. Luke 24:50-53.

27. See these creeds and others from church history at http://www.creeds.net/.

28. Acts 8:1.

29. 1 Corinthians 15:8.

30. Acts 1:3.

## Chapter 13—The Followers of Jesus

1. Gary Habermas, in an interview on "A Response to ABC's the Search for Jesus," on *The John Ankerberg Show,* 2001.

2. Lee Strobel, *The Case for Christ* (Grand Rapids, MI: Zondervan, 1998), p. 247.

3. J.P. Moreland, cited in Lee Strobel, *The Case for Christ* (Grand Rapids, MI: Zondervan, 1998), p. 247.

4. "After Jesus: the First Christians," *CNN,* at http://www.cnn.com/CNN/Programs/presents/after.jesus/.

5. All interview quotes in this chapter, unless otherwise noted, are from interviews on "A Response to ABC's the Search for Jesus," on *The John Ankerberg Show,* 2001.

6. N.T. Wright, in an interview on "A Response to ABC's the Search for Jesus," on *The John Ankerberg Show,* 2001.

7. F.F. Bruce, *The New Testament Documents: Are They Reliable?* (Grand Rapids, MI: Eerdmans Publishing, 1971), p. 46.

8. Ben Witherington, in an interview on "A Response to ABC's the Search for Jesus," on *The John Ankerberg Show,* 2001.

9. David Hume, *An Enquiry Concerning Human Understanding* (Oxford: Clarendon Press, 1902), p. 114.

10. Matthew 28:17 (emphasis added).

11. Darrell Bock, in an interview on "A Response to ABC's the Search for Jesus," on *The John Ankerberg Show,* 2001.

## Conclusion: What Should I Do with Jesus?

1. From "A Response to ABC's the Search for Jesus," on *The John Ankerberg Show,* 2001.

2. Isaiah 53:6 NLT.

3. Isaiah 59:2 NLT.

4. Ezekiel 18:4.

5. Matthew 25:31-46; John 5:21-29.

6. Isaiah 53:6 NLT.

7. Isaiah 53:5 NLT.

8. Isaiah 53:12 NLT.

9. 1 Peter 3:18 NLT.

10. Isaiah 55:6-7 NLT.

11. John 5:24 NLT.

12. John 17:3 NLT.

13. Ephesians 2:8-9 NLT.

## Appendix A

1. Adapted from John Ankerberg and John Weldon, *The Passion and the Empty Tomb* (Eugene, OR: Harvest House Publishers, 2005), pp. 185-91.

2. Gary Habermas, in an interview on "A Response to ABC's the Search for Jesus," on *The John Ankerberg Show*, 2001.

3. William Lane Craig, in an interview on "A Response to ABC's the Search for Jesus," on *The John Ankerberg Show*, 2001.

4. William Lane Craig, *The Son Rises: Historical Evidence for the Resurrection of Jesus* (Chicago: Moody Press, 1981), p. 102.

5. Gary Habermas, *Ancient Evidence for the Life of Jesus: Historical Records of His Death and Resurrection* (New York: Nelson, 1984), pp. 20-21.

## Appendix B

1. John Wenham, *The Easter Enigma* (Eugene, OR: Wipf & Stock Publishers, 2005).

2. Ibid., p. 87.

3. Gleason Archer, *Encyclopedia of Bible Difficulties* (Grand Rapids, MI: Zondervan, 1982), pp. 347-48.

4. Wenham, *The Easter Enigma*, pp. 81-82.

## Appendix C

1. Darrell Bock, "Hollywood Hype: The Oscars and Jesus' Family Tomb, What Do They Share?" February, 26, 2007. Accessed at http://dev.bible.org/bock/.

2. From Joel Rosenberg, "New Film Claims Jesus Didn't Rise from the Dead, Body Has Been Found," February 25, 2007. Accessed at http://joelrosenberg.blogspot.com/.

3. Ibid.

4. Ibid.

5. Ben Witherington, "The Jesus Tomb? Titanic Talpiot Tomb Theory Sunk from the Start," February 26, 2007. Accessed at http://www.johnankerberg.org/Articles/historical-Jesus/the-Jesus-family-tomb/the-Jesus-family-tomb-witherington-response.htm.

6. Michael Easley, John Ankerberg, Dillon Burroughs, *The Da Vinci Code Controversy* (Chicago: Moody, 2006).

7. Ben Witherington, "The Jesus Tomb? Titanic Talpiot Tomb Theory

Sunk from the Start," February 26, 2007. Accessed at http://www. johnankerberg.org/Articles/historical-Jesus/the-Jesus-family-tomb/the-Jesus-family-tomb-witherington-response.htm.

8. Darrell Bock, "Hollywood Hype: The Oscars and Jesus' Family Tomb, What Do They Share?" February, 26, 2007. Accessed at http://dev.bible.org/bock/.

9. Karen Matthews, "Documentary Shows Possible Jesus Tomb," *AP News*, February 26, 2007. Accessed at http://news.yahoo.com/s/ap/20070226/ap_on_re_us/jesus_s_burial.

10. Ibid.

11. Darrell Bock, "Hollywood Hype: The Oscars and Jesus' Family Tomb, What Do They Share?" February, 26, 2007. Accessed at http://dev.bible.org/bock/.

## About the Authors

**John Ankerberg,** host of the award-winning *John Ankerberg Show,* has three earned degrees: a Master of Arts in church history and the philosophy of Christian thought, a Master of Divinity from Trinity International University, and a Doctor of Ministry from Luther Rice Seminary. With Dr. John Weldon, he has coauthored *What Do Mormons Really Believe?, Fast Facts on Islam,* the "Facts on" Series of apologetic booklets, and other resources.

**Dillon Burroughs,** a full-time writer who has worked with a number of bestselling authors, is a graduate of Dallas Theological Seminary and coauthor of *Middle East Meltdown* (middleeastmeltdown.com) with John Ankerberg. He lives with his wife, Deborah, and their two children in Tennessee.

HARVEST HOUSE
PUBLISHERS